7.99

THE DIARY OF A CANNY MAN

1.   Adam Mackie, 1788–1850

THE DIARY OF A CANNY MAN, 1818–28.

Adam Mackie, Farmer, Merchant and Innkeeper in Fyvie

compiled by
WILLIAM MACKIE

edited with an introduction by
DAVID STEVENSON

ABERDEEN UNIVERSITY PRESS
Member of Maxwell Macmillan Publishing Corporation

First published 1991
Aberdeen University Press

British Library Cataloguing in Publication Data

Mackie, Adam
    The diary of a canny man, 1818–28 : Adam Mackie,
    farmer, merchant and innkeeper in Fyvie.
    I. Title   II. Mackie, William
    III. Stevenson, David, *1942–*
    941.2

ISBN 0 08 041213 0

Typeset by Hewer Text Composition Services
Printed by Athenaeum Press Ltd.

FOREWORD

This book stands as a memorial to two men—to Adam Mackie, whose fascinating diary of rural life in North East Scotland in the early nineteenth century provides a graphic picture of a world which has long since disappeared; and to Colonel William Mackie, his great-grandson, whose labours in transcribing and arranging material from the diaries have resulted in bringing his ancestor 'back to life'. But sadly, just as his dream of publishing Adam's work was about to reach fruition, Colonel Mackie died suddenly in 1989.

Adam Mackie (1788–1850), lived in the parish of Fyvie in Aberdeenshire, and prospered through his success in a wide range of activities—farming, innkeeping, dealing in illicit whisky, acting as a local bank agent, and above all, through his work as a shopkeeper and merchant serving the local community, procuring goods from Aberdeen and elsewhere to meet local needs, buying up the produce of small farmers in rural areas for transport to Aberdeen and other markets for sale. He was a man who could justifiably be proud of the standing he achieved in his community. But what makes him a figure of great interest to the historian is the remarkably full diary he kept from 1818 to 1828. Reflecting his unusually wide range of activities and interests, these provide insights into a great many aspects of rural life—personal, cultural and commercial—in Aberdeenshire. Most of the entries, written on a day to day basis, record incidents and tasks, usual and unusual, of daily life, but on occasion he reflects at length on a wide range of activities—his own successes and failures (personal and financial), his character, his family, the relationship of man and God, domestic and international political and economic developments.

That much of Adam's diaries is now being made available to readers is, as already noted, due to the work of Colonel William Mackie. Colonel Mackie was for many years fascinated by his ancestor's diary, which had remained in the family's possession. He made and arranged copious extracts from the diaries, and in 1972 he agreed that the diaries themselves should be microfilmed and copies deposited in the Scottish Record Office in Edinburgh and in Aberdeen University Library. He was again in touch with the SRO in 1989, and indicated that he hoped to have the material from the diary that he had edited published in book form—though he was uncertain whether he would ever find a publisher who shared his fascination with Adam Mackie.

At this point Dr Frances Shaw of the SRO suggested that Colonel Mackie get in touch with me, in my capacity (at that time) as Director of the Centre for Scottish Studies of the University of Aberdeen, as she knew that the Centre was active in publishing materials relating to the history of Northern Scotland. A reading of the typescript Colonel Mackie sent me indicated that it was indeed well worth publication: it was of great potential value not only to Adam's descendents through family piety, but to all interested in the social history of Scotland, and of the North East in particular. For this reason, I concluded that it would fit in well with the occasional series on Scottish studies sponsored by the Centre and published by Aberdeen University Press.

Colonel Mackie sent me his text in late August 1989, and though I promptly sent him an encouraging reply, it was not until 7 November that I was able to write confirming that the Centre would be prepared to undertake the editorial work necessary to ready the text for publication, and that AUP had agreed to be publisher. Sadly, Colonel Mackie had died suddenly on 12 October, at the age of 81, and thus never heard that the project which he had laboured on for so many years was to be completed.

However, with the aid of Colonel Mackie's eldest son (Adam's great great grandson), Graeme Mackie, work continued on preparation for publication. Right up to the time of his death Colonel Mackie had been juggling with the text, seeking to find the best way in which to present the material he had culled from the diary. He had recognised early on that publication of the complete text was impractical, for inevitably many of the entries are repetitious, narrating daily routines. Luckily, just a month before he died, he provided me with an answer to a crucial question about his typescript which only he could give. I had told him it would be essential for the reader to know how much of the full text was contained in his extracts, and the principles on which the extracts he had chosen were selected: 'Am I correct in thinking "all the most interesting, dramatic and unusual, plus a representative selection of the more routine and mundane items?"' He replied that the material selected for publication represented about half of the full text of the diary, and that 'Your views on the principles of selection of extracts are quite correct'. Invaluably, he then added a list giving a rough estimate of what proportion of the material relating to various subjects he had chosen for publication. Since then I have suppressed a few of the passages which he had chosen, as they seemed unduly repetitive, and added rather more, where interesting material had been omitted. Allowing for this, the extracts published below represent very approximately the following proportions of the total text of the manuscript diary.

All or nearly all:	children's education; Adam's reading; butter competitions; hawking; royal occasions; murder.
Well over half:	family; business reports and financial affairs; whisky; bee keeping; medical matters; local affairs; foreign affairs; religious views; economic views.
About half:	leisure and entertainment; public affairs.
Well under a half:	shopkeeping; innkeeping; farming.
About $\frac{1}{20}$th:	sermons.

Editorial decisions relating to the shortening of historical manuscripts for publication inevitably reflect the personal interests and the prejudices of the editor as well as those of the age and culture in which he lives: the above list will allow readers to see what judgements have been made as to priorities, and thus what distortions of the balance of the full text have been brought about by editing the diary. The most obvious one is the way in which Adam's reports on sermons are so severely cut. Another culture might find this scandalous: the average late twentieth-century reader is likely to be greatly relieved, even though (as the sample reports printed below demonstrate) Adam's comments are terse and intelligent.

What to select for publication from a text too long or too repetitive to present in full is one major decision for an editor. Another, in the case of a diary like Adam's, is how to arrange the extracts gleaned from the text. A simple chronological approach has much to recommend it: it preserves the order of the manuscript, and it is true to the way life is lived, with events personal, family and of wider import, trivial and portentous, ludicrous and tragic, jumbled up together. But such an approach can also seem to present a random chaos to the reader, with themes and threads of development concealed in life's daily confusions. An alternative is therefore an analytical approach, gathering together material bearing on individual subjects and themes. This is the approach Colonel Mackie chose to adopt. Its strength is that it provides fascinating sections on related themes and events. But, as he clearly recognised, there is the problem that even a single sentence from the diary sometimes has claims to inclusion in several different sections, and adjudicating between rival claims can be difficult and lead to unavoidable inconsistencies.

In the introduction which follows I have made use of material contained in drafts of an introduction written by Colonel Mackie, and information supplied by Graeme Mackie. Most of the details concerning Adam's life after the diary ends in 1828 have been extracted from what he titled his 'Stock and Inventory Book', which has miscellaneous entries covering the years 1836-50.

The hand in which Adam Mackie wrote his diaries is generally clear and presents few problems. But his lack of punctuation and erratic capitalisation leaves the editor to supply the one and regularise the other. Even so, occasionally Adam is somewhat incoherent and ungrammatical, but his wording has been retained, sometimes with a word or words added in square brackets to clarify his meaning. Minor errors of spelling have been silently corrected, and abbreviations expanded

The microfilms of Adam Mackie's diaries deposited in the Scottish Record Office have been classified there as RH.4/66/1-7. The same reel also holds Adam's Stock and Inventory Book,—RH.4/66/8,—and the indenture of his apprenticeship which is reproduced in Appendix I,—RH.4/66/9. The extracts from the process papers relating to the trial of William Allan for murder in 1825, which appear in Appendix II, are taken from SRO, JC.8/19, and appear with the approval of the Keeper of the Records of Scotland.

It was Colonel Mackie's intention that after he had completed work on the diaries they should be deposited for safe-keeping in Aberdeen University Library, and since his death his son Graeme Mackie has arranged for their deposit on permanent loan: they are now classified as AUL MS 3347.

In the draft foreword which Colonel Mackie had prepared for this volume he expressed his thanks to the staff of the Scottish Record Office and Aberdeen University Library for their help in dealing with his enquiries relating to the projected publication of the diary over the years.

FOREWORD

My own thanks go to Graeme Mackie, for providing information for use in the introduction and reading over the final text, correcting many minor errors in the process. Illustrations 1 and 2 are from originals in the possession of Graeme Mackie, while 3–5 are from the George Washington Wilson Collection in Aberdeen University Library.

DAVID STEVENSON
Department of Scottish History
University of St Andrews

CONTENTS

INTRODUCTION

Adam Mackie was born in the rural Aberdeenshire parish of Fyvie on the 3rd of January, 1788. His father, also named Adam, combined farming at Mains of Fyvie with the trade of shoemaker. A picture of the parish as it was while Adam was growing up can be obtained from the entry for Fyvie in the *Statistical Account of Scotland*, compiled in 1793 by William Moir, the parish minister. Much of the parish consisted of bare moorlands, though their nakedness was in places being covered by plantations of trees. The cultivated land of the parish produced 'pretty good' early crops of oats and bear (barley), the land being being 'generally kindly', especially near the church and castle. Fashionable—and potentially highly profitable—improvements in farming practices were spreading in the parish, most farmers growing some turnips and potatoes, and sowing grasses and clover. The old Scots plough was used only on very stony ground: elsewhere the lighter 'English' plough had generally been adopted, though usually drawn by traditional teams of eight to ten oxen, four-horse teams being in a minority.

The people of the parish had their minister's approval: they were

> in general decent and well behaved; seldom frequenting the inn or tavern, but upon very particular occasions; generally sympathizing with those in distress, and ready to give them such assistance as they can afford. Their houses are in general more neat and comfortable than they were 30 years ago. Their dress and manner of living are also improved.

The only industry in the parish thought worthy of note by Moir was the spinning of wool and knitting it into hose, the many women employed in this trade receiving the wool from Aberdeen merchants who subsequently collected the end product. In addition some men servants (labourers) knitted their own stockings on winter evenings, 'a much better way of employing their time than frequenting the ale-house, of which there are only three in the parish'. Tradesmen in the parish included nine shoemakers (Adam's father being one), ten weavers, seven smiths, ten tailors, eleven wrights and two dyers—and a midwife 'regularly bred to the business' by the kirk session.

At the centre of the parish's life was the parish kirk—though there were several hundred 'dissenters', mainly episcopalians, in the population of about 2,200. Near the church lay the school, of which Mr Moir was clearly proud:

> the education of youth is at present carried on at this school on the most approved plan; besides what is generally taught at grammar schools, the French and English languages are taught here with as much purity and exactness as in most of the English academies . . .a circumstance which deserves to be remarked, as few country parishes enjoy the like advantage.

How much did the success and breadth of interests of Adam Mackie owe to his training in this school?

In the 1790s the land of the parish of Fyvie was owned by eight landlords, but only three of them were resident. The most important of the proprietors, from the point of view of the Mackie family, was the Honourable General William Gordon of Fyvie, whose mains (or home) farm was rented by Adam's father and whose seat, Fyvie Castle, stood adjacent to the farm—though the general was only occasionally in residence.

This was the little world into which Adam Mackie was born. In human terms a world of tenant farmers and their servants, tradesmen, spinsters and knitters, with an élite of landlords a presence at once dominant and distant. Physically it was a world of cultivated fields surrounded by heath-covered moors, through which the little River Ythan wound its way past the castle and the marshes which almost surrounded it. The castle represented civil power, the parish church religious authority, with the remains of the medieval priory hinting at an older faith. Another reminder of wider worlds was provided by the main road from Aberdeen to Banff which passed through the parish, bearing the carts of traders and the mail coaches.

Adam studied at the parish school, but little is known of his childhood—though he later recorded that when he was ten years old he had herded cows for one of the smaller landowners in the parish, Mr James Hay of Monkshill. Though first known to Adam as an employer, Mr Hay was later to become a friend and respected adviser as Adam moved on to better things: Hay may well have recognised Adam's energy and abilities and encouraged his aspirations. Adam's father intended that his son should follow him in the family trade of shoemaker, and in 1800, at the age of twelve, Adam was apprenticed to his uncle, William Mackie, shoemaker in Aberdeen (see Appendix I). Adam served the five years of his apprenticeship, but it is frustrating to know nothing more than this of his life in these years. What did he learn beyond how to make boots, in the bustling and fast-developing commercial city of Aberdeen? The experience cannot have failed to widen his horizons, and judging by his later appetite for knowledge (not least of the multifarious ways of making money) he doubtless took full advantage of the opportunities living in Aberdeen brought him.

Yet Adam returned to Fyvie at the end of his apprenticeship in 1805, and even though he was to abandon the trade in which he had been trained he never seems to have considered leaving Fyvie. In spite of his ambitions, he saw Fyvie and the surrounding parishes as offering him the opportunities for advancement that he craved. In 1815 he achieved independence by renting the farm of Lewes of Fyvie, perhaps with financial help from his father. In the years that followed Adam showed much energy in improving the farm, rebuilding the steading and the field dykes, and taking advantage of the opportunities offered by the farm's position on the main road through the parish to branch out into shopkeeping and innkeeping, and using the shop as a collecting point for hosiery knitted by the local 'wives'.

By 1817 Adam was sufficiently well established to marry his cousin and housekeeper, Mary Jameson—who was already pregnant—something so common in this rural society that no particular scandal would have been caused by it. Nor would the fact that Adam's earlier relationship with one Rachel Gordon had produced an illegitimate son have aroused very much comment. Adam gave the boy his own name, and this younger Adam was brought up along with Mary's children, his half brothers and sisters.

It is at this point in his life that Adam began his diaries. Why? Partly because he was proud of his success and wished to record it. But keeping such a diary fitted in well with other traits of his character: his love of order and systematic recording and calculating. He believed a diary would help him organise the enterprise of his own life and provide a spur to reflection on both his own conduct and on wider issues. It would, he hoped, help him change his ways, in that both the act of writing and the act of later re-reading would draw his attention to his own failings. The 'journal diary', as he called it, was to be on the one hand his servant, an aide-mémoire: but it was also to be his 'taskmaster', calling him to account for how he spent his time, that precious but all too limited commodity which marched inexorably on. Adam was keenly aware of the brevity of the human life-span, and he saw wasting time as his major personal failing. A taskmaster-diary would, he hoped, save him from idleness and complacency. His success in business had removed the spur of necessity to make him work hard, but he was morally convinced that he should continue to work hard. Revealingly, one of the very few axioms relating to conduct which he recorded from his reading was that even if one could afford luxury one should resist indulging in it, for ease enervates the mind and 'overcomes the whole frame'.

Increasingly Adam's time was spent not working on the land—his 'man' or servant organised this under his supervision—but in serving in the shop or the 'house', his public house or bar. Both provided opportunities for slipping into ease and time-wasting. In the bar there was the temptation to gossip and drink with customers he knew. In the shop there were slack times when there were no customers to serve, yet he had to be available in case any appeared. He usually managed to fill in such time gainfully: drawing up his accounts; unpacking goods brought from Aberdeen merchants; packing goods to take with him for sale or barter on the days he went out on his rounds collecting eggs and butter; packing the eggs and curing the butter for dispatch to Aberdeen; repairing and cleaning the shop and other buildings; working in his garden; tending his beehives. But nonetheless he felt the frustration of being almost imprisoned by the shop, the pettiness of many of the tasks with which he filled his time, and sometimes when he came to write up the day in his diary he felt that much of his time had been wasted day-dreaming, or reading the paper while waiting for customers—though at least that could be regarded as improving.

Yet the diary is not dominated by such frustrations and dissatisfaction with his own conduct. On the contrary, he repeatedly calls himself a contented man. At times, as when he lists his financial successes with pride and points out how much better he has done than his contemporaries, he could even be called a self-satisfied man. But this is balanced by his acknowledgement that he is a very lucky man: his success may owe much to his own abilities, but without luck and the goodness of God he could have achieved nothing. And though some aspects of his work brought frustration, it brought him and his family a good living, and he did get out regularly on his rounds in the countryside bartering for eggs and butter, or visiting Aberdeen to deal with the merchants there. These days were probably the ones he regarded as the most rewarding in his working life.

Adam liked money: it was the measure of his success, and it was this aspect of money rather than the spending-power it gave him which drove him on to further acquisition of it. But possession of money in itself was not necessarily meritorious. It had to be money honestly earned. This is a theme Adam returned to on several occasions. He offered fair prices when buying and asked fair prices when selling, in accordance with the state of the market, and avoided haggling. Of course we have no direct way of knowing whether the customers in his shop or the farmers' wives selling him eggs would have shared this assessment of Adam's business morality. But the circumstantial evidence that he was regarded as a fair dealer is strong: they voted with their feet by continuing to deal with him, though there were a number of rivals they could have taken their custom to.

Adam Mackie was proud of his success: but he probably only confided this to his diary—and perhaps his wife. Otherwise he was evidently content to let his success speak for itself. As well as being satisfied with his success, Adam was engagingly surprised by it. As he repeatedly pointed out, the country was in the midst of serious agricultural depression, prices of grain and cattle had collapsed at the end of the Napoleonic Wars in 1815. Farmers were hard hit, and nearly all his customers were men and women dependant on the land for their living. Yet he thrived—though haunted by the idea that he could have been doing much better, if prices for agricultural produce were higher and his customers therefore better-off. The secret of his success lay partly in his own personal qualities of hard work careful planning, and a good eye and ear for new opportunities to exploit. Diversification seems to have been his watchword. He had so many irons in the fire that difficulties on the farming side of his business through low prices were more than compensated for elsewhere. Shopkeeper; buyer of eggs and butter, with a hand also in the sale of locally-made cloth to Aberdeen cloth merchants; butter maker; beekeeper; innkeeper, selling drink and taking in lodgers, and dealer in illicit whisky. 'General merchant' is the only term which even comes near to encompassing his activities.

A fair man; a contented man; a busy man (in spite of his self-criticism on this score); an ambitious man—though only within the narrow sphere of his rural parish. In many respects a very conventional man, as is demonstrated, paradoxically, by the instances on which he does defy the regulations of church and state, for in all respects his deviations are ones which were quite acceptable in the society in which he lived. With an illegitimate son and a pregnant bride he failed to live up to the ideals of his religion, but this did not seem to worry him or anyone else particularly as such sins were commonplace. In his diary he noted many illegitimate births and pregnant brides, but did not condemn them, except where such lapses were seen as particularly irresponsible given the circumstances of those concerned. The bride who missed her wedding breakfast through giving birth was perhaps seen as guilty of bad planning as much as anything else. Fornication in his own house - whether involving servant and servant or servant and lodger—he would not tolerate, but not through moral outrage as much as through belief that even if one accepted such lapses it would be wrong to condone them. Where the law of the land was concerned, Adam was law-abiding except where in the eyes of society the law was even more of an ass than usual. When rivals invoked a law against hawkers which had not previously been enforced to try to spoil his trade, Adam was initially downhearted at having to pay fines, rather than because he felt guilty. He rallied quickly once he found that publicity and sympathy were increasing his sales. His customers clearly shared his opinion of the law. Adam would have agreed, in this case at least, with the saying that no publicity is bad publicity. As to the laws relating to distilling, like the great majority of the population he ignored them as far as possible. Luckily the excise officials responsible for trying to enforce the impractical regulations often drank or lodged in his house, which gave Adam good opportunities to keep track of their movements. When the law changed and the trade declined, Adam's reaction was to invest in a now legal distillery.

Adam was unperturbed by buying and selling illicit whisky under the noses of those responsible for suppressing the trade. As this indicates, there was much of the phlegmatic in his character. The matter-of-fact tone of much of the diary reflects this; on the whole his writing is calm and controlled, often strictly factual. Though the near coincidence of the new year and his own birthday (3 January) inspired him to introspective bouts of analysis and reflection, these are of a rational and measured sort. He is sincere in chiding himself for his idleness; he is heartfelt in his expressions of religious belief as he applied the lessons of the sermons he carefully listened to and summarised each week. But passion, whether of joy or agony, is rare. He recorded his satisfaction in having an agreeable wife, whom he could talk to both when things were going well and when they were not; and he missed her when she was away for a few days. But that is about all he has to say on that subject. When passion does break through, as when he recorded having sat and watched his little daughter die a lingering death in agony, and being utterly helpless to do anything to help, it is all the more moving for being so rare.

Adam Mackie very much fits the modern definition of being the type of man who defines himself, gives himself meaning and place in society, through the work he does. But he was also a man who found time for socialising and recreation. Dinner or tea with friends and relatives, especially on Sunday, in his house or theirs. Drinking with cronies whom he was serving in 'the house', thus combining work and recreation. Sometimes the price to be paid for such social drinking was admitted to—a hangover the next morning. Adam was also an omnivorous reader, buying himself an encyclopedia but also reading anything that came to hand, from the principles of gas lighting to the life of the Devil. The only time a pattern emerges in his book-reading was when, having read one of Walter Scott's Waverley novels, he raced through a number of others in quick succession.

The strongest influences in determining Adam's outlook on the world at large were the two Aberdeen newspapers, the *Journal* and the *Chronicle*, which he read avidly in evenings, on the Sabbath, or when business was slack in the shop. Foreign wars made him bless the peace the country enjoyed—though at one point he indicated that a foreign war would be no bad thing, as it would lead to a recovery in prices of agricultural produce. As well as pondering the great issues of the day in the outside world, he showed a very human appetite for gossip and scandal—he revels in the details of the abortive attempt of George IV to divorce Queen Caroline. A local murder provided sensational events virtually on his own doorstep, and a chance to visit Edinburgh through being called as a witness in the subsequent trial. Typically, Adam took charge of the travel arrangements for the witnesses from Fyvie, and as a result they all enjoyed a profit when their expenses were paid.

Adam recorded that he began his diary in June, 1819, and this is the date given on the title page of the first volume. Yet the first entry is dated 1 May, 1818. Perhaps his 1818 resolution to keep a diary was abortive, and he made a new start in June, 1819, copying what earlier notes he had into the volume. Certainly it is notable that the second entry in the diary, immediately following his declaration that he is going to keep a 'taskmaster', is different from any subsequent entry in that it tells us nothing of Adam's life or attitudes—it is a little essay on the Water of Methlick: perhaps it took him time to learn how to keep a diary, to decide what type of material it was appropriate to record.

The diary ends with a routine entry—for 28 February, 1828—and no explanation. It is possible of course that he continued his diary, but that subsequent volumes have been lost. That the final entry is on the last page of the seventh of the little volumes which comprise the diary might suggest this. On the other hand, however, most of that last page is blank, which is contrary to his practice in the other six volumes. Perhaps it was simply that after ten years Adam tired of diary-keeping, and looking through it realised how repetitive many of the entries were. Coming to the end of a volume, he may have he realised that he could not be bothered starting another one. But it is known that some of his papers have been lost, for his 'Stock and Inventory Book', which has entries for 1836–50, contains a reference to his 'foregoing inventory book', of which there is now no trace.

However, the surviving stock book tells us a good deal about Adam's later life, for it consists of a miscellany of estimates of his financial position and copies or drafts of important papers, such as his own will. The book indicates that Adam continued to prosper. In time he lent quite substantial sums of money to the lairds of Fyvie (his own landlords) and other landowners in the neighbourhood, and his financial activities also expanded through his appointment as agent in Fyvie for the Aberdeen Town and Country Banking Corporation in 1838, at an annual salary of £30. In 1843 he not only renewed the lease of Lewes for twenty-one years, but took over the tenancy of the farm of Petty for a similar term. Adam's steadily increasing prosperity received a check, however, at the time of the financial crash of 1848: his investments in Aberdeen banks and in two American companies were hard hit. But though he sustained substantial losses, at the end of 1849 he estimated his worth in property, goods and investments at £7,100. He died on 22 May, 1850.

Adam Mackie's first wife, Mary Jameson, bore him one more child after the end of the period covered by the diary, James, born in 1832. In February, 1835 Mary died at the age of thirty-five, and on 24 August, 1836 Adam took as his second wife Isabella Rose. Adam had been a friend of her father, David Rose, tollkeeper at Fyvie, who had died in 1826. Adam had done what he could to help Isabella—the 'Bell' of the diary—and her sister after their father died, and now she came to Adam's help when he was bereaved. By Bell Adam had four more children, David (born 1836); Mary (born 1838 and died 1840); Sarah (born 1840); and Mary (born 1841 and died 1852). Thus Adam was survived by all his children except the first two Marys (one by each of his wives)—though the third of the Marys was also to die in childhood.

In providing for his family in the event of his death, Adam showed typical careful calculation—though also indecision. In March, 1835, just after his first wife's death, he planned that his surviving children—including the illegitimate Adam—should receive £800 each. His second marriage complicated this, and Adam was clearly determined that his re-marriage should not prejudice the prospects of his children. By law a widow could claim a 'terce', a third of her deceased husband's heritable property—land and buildings— and a share of his moveable property, unless she surrendered such rights. On 5 August, 1835 Adam had his bride-to-be sign such an agreement. On his death she would receive only an annuity of £10 a year, plus an extra £1 a year for each year the marriage had lasted before Adam's death—up to a maximum annuity of £20. If she re-married, or forfeited her moral character, she would not even be entitled to this. In addition, she was to be entitled to £30 of household furniture and linen, plus £5 to pay for mourning. The rest of his estate was to be divided equally between his children.

However, Adam soon decided he had been a bit mean: the annuity would be 'barely sufficient to maintain her in a manner similar to what has been customary in my family'. He therefore decided that she should have a lump sum of £50 on his death as well as the annuity. He calculated that this would leave about £4,000 to be divided among his five children. Rather oddly, Adam noted that if he lived a few more years he intended to transform this draft of his intentions into a legal will. When he had such a clear picture of how he intended to distribute his estate, why the delay? Part of the answer doubtless lay in the fact that he foresaw the birth of children by his second wife, so realised that further adjustments would be necessary. He waited until all four children of his second marriage had been born before recording his revised plans for his property. He then wrote into his stock-book a 'Draught sketch of intended will and testament'. All his household furniture and goods, and bed and table linen, were to go to his widow, Bell, together with the annuity previously specified. Six of his children (Margaret, William, James, David, Sarah and Mary) were to receive £750 or goods to that value, and William was also to inherit the tenancy of Petty, less the value of its stock and equipment. James was to receive Lewes on the same terms, and take over the merchant's business, less the value of goods in the shop or in stock. George was to receive £650, £100 less than the other legitimate children, 'in consequence of heavy expenditure on his education'—he had gone to university. Adam's eldest son and namesake, however, was only to get £300, as his father regarded him as 'not entitled to quite half as much as the others in consequence of him having withdrawn himself so long from my family'.

This withdrawal had taken the form of emigration to the United States in 1835, where Adam junior became a lawyer and practised in New Bedford, Massachusetts. Perhaps the awkwardness of being the eldest child of the family but illegitimate had led young Adam to distance himself from the rest of the family in this way. Perhaps too memories of the brutal floggings he had received at school made Fyvie a place of unhappy memories—though he had subsequently been awarded the school's annual bursary of £2.10s., and later, it is said, he sent his own eldest son, another Adam, back to Fyvie from America to be taught the correct pronunciation of Latin!

Of the other children of Adam the diarist, Margaret evidently never married, and lived at Lewes until her death in 1876, along with her step-grandmother, Jane Nicol, the second wife of the diarist's father, who lived on until 1882. Sarah married a farmer from near Peterhead and little is known of her subsequent life. William farmed at Petty until his death in 1897. In 1877 he was presented with a massive Family Bible by his fellow Sabbath School teachers, in recognition of his very long service. George, after qualifying as a doctor at Aberdeen University, subsequently became a well-known general practitioner in the Insch area of Aberdeenshire.

James, the diarist's third legitimate son, bought the stock of the shop from his father in 1850, being given interest-free credit by the latter until he could pay—presumably out of the shop's profits, and it was intended he should buy the shop as well. But within a few months Adam was dead, and James inherited both shop and the tenancy of Lewes. Though he gave up innkeeping, his mind, like his father's, was ever on expansion. He converted the business into a limited liability company, James Mackie and Co. Ltd. (all the shareholders being members of the family), and set up branches throughout Aberdeenshire—and even one in Dundee, mainly as an outlet for butter and eggs.

David, the eldest son by the diarist's second marriage, qualified in medicine at Aberdeen University, like his half-brother George. He joined the Indian Medical Service, and had the distinction of being the first to suggest that the sandfly was the insect vector for propagating the causative organism of the tropical disease Kala-Azar or sandfly fever.

So far as is known, Adam did not sign a formal will until 1849, a year before his death. Its terms were very similar to those he had drafted more than a decade before. Bell was to get her £20 annuity, £5 for mourning, £30 of household furnishings, and a £50 legacy, though she would forfeit the annuity on remarriage or loss of moral character, it passing to his daughter Margaret. The younger Adam continued to be penalised for emigrating to the United States. He was to have £300, provided there were sufficient funds to give all his other children double that sum, 'because I wish not to send money abroad and leave poverty at home'. The rest of his personal property was to be divided equally among his seven other surviving children. If, instead of realising investments and taking their legacies in cash, the children decided to take over existing investments, the whole property was to be divided into what were, at current values at the time of division, equal lots, and a draw was to be organised, with a stranger—'say a child of about ten years'—drawing tickets assigning lots to the various children. The legacies of the younger children were not to be made over to them until they reached the age of twenty-one. As to the two farms Adam leased, William was to get Petty (which he already worked). As next son in age George might seem to be due Lewes, but he was pursuing the medical profession which 'does not seem in accordance with the practical occupation of land', so the farm would pass to James.

Finally, Adam recommended that his children live together in families, with the females putting themselves under the protection of the males, making 'themselves as agreeable to each other as they can'. Thus Adam the family man was concerned not merely to provide materially for his children, but to do what he could to preserve harmony by treating them fairly and equally, and to have them continue as a family unit until the younger children reached adulthood. Adam reveals the common human yearning to legislate for developments after his death, and an awareness of how strong was the tendency for families to fall out in disputes over inheritance. Under this will, when Adam died in 1850 his seven children still in Scotland inherited nearly £1,000 each. (Scottish Record Office, SC.1/36/27, pp.1179–210, and SC.1/37/27, pp.1567–80).

Adam the diarist was buried in Fyvie, and lies there surrounded by some of his children, grand-children and great grandchildren. Many of his descendants are still living, though none now live in Fyvie. He was a man proud of his success in life, and of his status in his community. Through publication of much of his diary, knowledge of his life and reflections on it will reach a much wider audience. Who can doubt that knowledge of this would have given him satisfaction?—but a contentment to be quietly confided to a diary, not boasted about overmuch in public.

Adam's diaries descended to his eldest son, James, and in due course to James's eldest son, also called James. Colonel William Mackie, whose work on the diaries has led to their publication, was the third son of this younger James. William's two elder brothers died childless, and thus he inherited the diaries from his father.

Born in 1908, William Mackie was educated at the grammar school in Turriff, and then followed his great-uncle David by studying medicine at Aberdeen University. Like David, William had his eye on the Indian Medical Service, but regulations required him to serve as a general practitioner before entry. This brought him a wife as well as practical experience: he acted as assistant to Dr James Taylor in Keith, and in due course married the latter's daughter, Isabel.

In India William rose to the rank of colonel at the comparatively early age of thirty-five, but returned to Scotland when India became independent in 1947. He had specialised in medical administration, and became successively medical superintendent of the Perthshire group of hospitals, and medical director of the Eastern Region hospitals. After retirement in 1969 William settled in Devon. There he at last had time to work seriously on his great-grandfather's diary. Without his work it would not be being published now.

PART 1

Adam: The Man And His Family

2.   Where Adam worshipped. Parish Church, Fyvie

Chapter 1

THE DIARY

1819
Number 1st
Diary Journal
commenced June 1819
by
Adam Mackie
Lewes of Fyvie

1st May, 1818

This book is purposed for writing down occurrences, passing events
and designed to serve as a refreshment of mind afterwards, and to
be a sort of diary wherein I may write what manner I have spent my
time whether in labour, study, business, pleasure or idleness. Also to
be a taskmaster which I may suppose asks the question every night:
What have you done this day?

31st December, 1819

This day finishes this book and also the present year 1819. I am in
good health myself and family and plenty of provender for man and
beast. Storm knee deep . . .

15th April, 1821

I now close a third number of my daily remarks since commencement near two years in June 1819. Myself and family are in health
at the moment and have plenty of the comforts and conveniences of
life for which may God accept my grateful acknowledgements and
continue those blessings.

16th April, 1821
I call this book the fourth number of my diary being the fourth in order since I commenced this regulation in June 1819 now near two years. Myself and family are at present in good health and in circumstance comfortable.

22nd February, 1823
This ends another part of my diary continued since June 1819 and which I mean to continue as long as I have health which at present (thank God) I perfectly enjoy.

23rd February, 1823
At the commencement of a new part of my daily memorandums, it may not be amiss to say (as I already did in June, 1819) what are my reasons for continuing these remarks, and first it gives a person a kind of information what they have been about and as we are all liable to misspend a considerable part of our time the misspent must stand something like a blank in the other ordinary affairs, but if there is no memorandum taken these blanks soon escape our memories and are certain portions of our time annihilated, whereas a review of the time lost may be a sufficient stimulus to a thinking person that now is the time for improving the present and as much as possible retrieving the past. The diary is also a kind of tract of a person's progress through the business of life, which tract does not close but continues so visible that a person can at any time see the dangers escaped, the difficulties surmounted, the success met with, and the reverses he has suffered. It is of further use as a memorandum book of public and private events that may be passing at the time. When we have the news of storms by sea or land in other places, my diary tells me what kind the weather was that day here, whether it be week, month, or year hence. A stranger to read these memorandums would be ready to say there is nothing of merit here, but shows that time has been allowed to pass unemployed and unimproved rather than to notice worthy actions which the vanity of the person thought he was doing, but every person considered in his own sphere, it is mine to keep in sight of my business as well as I can. Erudition I have no claim to, but to manage my little trade right is what I consider my duty, and this book is a faint representation of my proceedings. The daily remarks though trifling require attention to have them daily posted, for if allowed to fall much back it sets memory on the rack

to give an account of the bygone, and that account will most likely be imperfect.

14th August, 1824

Thus ends another week and with it another part of my diary in which on the whole there is little variety, my business being a continued round that makes a revolution every two weeks.

15th August, 1824

Begins a new part of my diary, which is a fresh notice to me that my days are fast passing away and these remarks serve to inform me that my time is but very middling laid out for the interests of this life, and still less for the interest of that which is to come, and that I am not using a half, a third, nor a fourth of the advantages I have for improving and establishing my soul in knowledge, wisdom, and righteousness. May God be pleased to give me Grace that I pass and employ every portion of my time aright that I may be comfortable here and assure the happiness of a hereafter.

12th March, 1826

At the commencement of another part of diary it may not be amiss to remark that myself, my wife and children are all in good health.

Chapter 2

FAMILY FORTUNES:
ADAM AND HIS HOUSEHOLD

19th July, 1818
I have got myself married to Mary Jameson, who hath been in the capacity of housekeeper to me since the 11th February, 1817, about a year and five months.

16th December, 1818
I have this day got my first daughter baptized by Mr Falconer in presence of David Rose, tollkeeper, and Alexander Ewen, my own boy. The name is Margaret and is one year and seven months younger than my boy (by Rachel Gordon) named Adam, who was born the 7th May, 1817, at Aberdeen.

19th August, 1819
. . . also made application to the minister for a second certificate to Rachel Gordon, which I got and sent her.

22nd August, 1819
Rachel Gordon here enquiring about a certificate from the [kirk] session, which was enclosed and sent to her on Thursday last.

5th October, 1819
Afternoon went and met the burial of William Mackie, James Mackie's oldest boy.

29th November, 1819
Wife out with the child Margaret at night getting her inoculated with the cowpox at James Carl's.

9 September, 1819
Terrible ill with a toothache.

11 September, 1819
I feel a little better of my tooth this morning but not a whole head altogether.

3rd January, 1820
This day if I am right informed is my birthday. I was born 3rd January, 1788 and am now thirty-two years of age, and when I reflect on the bypast part of my life, thirty-two years, which is considerable, it is passed as if unobserved and I may say unimproved. I think with the advantages I have had I might have a much better informed mind if I only would have employed my leisure hours, but I find myself given to ease and idleness and time passes imperceptibly away.

28th June, 1820
My wife complaining of uneasiness previous to her inlying. Have sent for the midwife, who arrived here by breakfast time.

29th June, 1820
My wife not much better but allows the midwife to go away . . . At night sends back for midwife. Mary finds herself worse and is in labour throughout the night, painful in the extreme.

30th June, 1820
Mary continues in the same extreme state of illness. After some thought and consideration of mind I proceed on my Auchterless journey . . . Have had a restless and uneasy mind about the situation of my wife. Had advice when leaving Redhill that all is well and delivered of a boy. When a little further on had advice that the mother is middling but the child dead, which turns out to be true.

27th August, 1820
My wife in company with Bell Rose off this morning in the mail coach to Old Meldrum to see her friends there. Myself reading and waiting at home.

4th December, 1820
A burial belonging [sic.] William Mackie, Aberdeen. A[t] churchyard went up and assisted off and on with gravestone.

3rd January, 1821
This is my birthday when I complete the 33rd year of my age, being born 3 January 1788. This I may say is the prime of my life and the best of my days. I am strong and in perfect health. My family are also all well.

12th October, 1821
Out at Auchterless . . . Ordered a man with a horse to meet me at Redhill, which he did and told me my wife was unwell. Came home as fast as I could and found her delivered of a girl before my arrival (at half past eight o'clock) and all in an ordinary way. Blessed be God who in mercy hath spared the mother and given a child with less labour than expected. May a sense of such goodness make a lasting impression on our minds that we walk worthy of the Lord in righteousness, wisdom and knowledge, and that we order our life and conversation so that God may be glorified, whose liberal hand hath also provided for us plentifully of the good things of this life. God grant that we may be forever enabled to bless thy name and do thy will.

20th October, 1821
Have got down the minister and baptized the child Mary.

2nd December, 1821
Had Dr Argo part of this evening, who was down seeing the boy's head.

3rd January, 1822
I this day complete the thirty-fourth year of my age. My wife is also twenty-eight years and about three months, being born October, 1793, whereby I am five years and nine months older than her.

18th March, 1822
Adam is sent to school this day for first time.

18th May, 1822
There is a marriage proposed the morrow between my brother, George Mackie, and my wife's sister, Betty Jameson. My wife is up there assisting at cooking.

19th May, 1822
As soon as I got myself ready, about ten o'clock, went up to George Mackie's as he intends being married after kirk time. I proposed some new arrangements of getting the ceremony put past before kirk time, which I succeeded in on applying to the minister and precentor. The bride arrived at the Manse after twelve o'clock about ten minutes, where they were immediately married . . . This afternoon I have spent with the marriage company that has consisted of about from thirty to forty people.

23rd May, 1822
Left the market about six o'clock and was home a little after seven, when I have notice that my mother has died this day about one o'clock. She has been in a poor state of health for some time back; for the last two weeks her health was thought considerably better.

25th May, 1822
My mother's funeral being this afternoon, made myself ready and went up there about three o'clock. The company consisted of about twenty-five men, who conversed and drank whisky punch until after five o'clock, and the body was laid down about six. My mother's name was Margaret Findlay. She was born at Cairnbrogy in the parish of Tarves. Her father's name was Peter Findlay, who had removed from Cairnbrogy to Ardconnon in the parish of Meldrum, where he died when my mother had been about eight or ten years of age. The widow, Margaret Barron, married again to a person of the name of Jameson, a widower also in Tulloch, same parish of Meldrum; and the late George Jameson, shoemaker in Old Meldrum, my wife's father, was a son of that marriage. By which means my wife and me are the son and daughter of half brother and sister. My mother is about seventy or seventy-two years of age at her death.

7th June, 1822
The children are ill with the chin cough.

23rd June, 1822
Took a walk this afternoon with the children and wife up the Den of Rothie. The children are ill in the chin cough.

29th June, 1822
My wife . . . proposing going to Peterhead on Monday together with the children.

1st July, 1822
I have been up early this morning sending my wife and children away to Peterhead. Got a seat erected in a cart and them ranked out and set off about seven o'clock.

7th July, 1822
Had my father at dinner and none else. I feel a little out of my element and lonely for want of the society of my wife who is at Peterhead.

11th July, 1822
I am making preparations for travel the morrow - erected a seat in a cart to send for my wife and family and coupled it over with hoops to suspend a cover.

13th July, 1822
Wife and family arrives from Peterhead about nine o'clock. The children are not yet clear of the chin cough but are otherwise all in good health and have got a fine day. I think I shall again feel comfortable in the society of my wife.

6th August, 1822
Have forbidden my boy Adam going to school in consequence of him receiving more discipline than instructions as I conceive, the impression of one flogging not being worn out until his backside is black with another; and this in a child four years of age is perhaps as hurtful to my feelings as to his body.

7th August, 1822

Mr Thain, the schoolmaster, called here and made an apology in regard to Adam my boy's treatment, and promises to be more attentive and less severe in his discipline in time coming and I have sent him back.

11th November, 1822

Have sent Mr Thain a half boll coals that came with the cart from Aberdeen—a present to stimulate his attention to Adam at the school.

3rd January, 1823

This day another year of my life is slipped away, this being the anniversary of my birthday, when I complete the thirty-fifth year of my age. I find myself in perfect health of body (and if I be sufficient judge of myself) the faculties of my mind are in their ordinary tone. My circumstances are such as makes my mind easy. The affairs of my house (a public one) with few exceptions goes smoothly on. My wife and children have health. I have peace in my family and I feel contented . . .

While I am sensible of the prosperity of my own affairs, I hope a sense thereof shall be preserved on my mind that while I am enjoying the good things of this life I may not neglect to give God the praise, who besides the success of business hath bestowed on me an agreeable wife to whom I can safely relieve my mind, whether joy or sorrow, with whom also I have the happiness of my comforts . . . divided.

2nd February, 1823

Had an invitation last night from my wife's sister, Margaret Jameson, Old Meldrum, to come in to her marriage the morrow, that is this day: which invitation was the less acceptable as it was in quick succession after we had been at one [marriage, on 1st February], and seems very unpromising weather, being thick and drifting snow. My wife insists that some of her friends from this should countenance her, on which account we get ourselves ready, by about 8 o'clock, with both horses, myself on one and man on the other and wife behind him: and after encountering some severe drifting storm get there by half past ten. Attended with the marriage at the chapel half before eleven. Was also kirked there the man (James Joss by name) being of that persuasion. After leaving the chapel, the party proceeded to the bridegroom's father's house about a half mile east of the chapel where we dined twelve or fifteen in number. Spent the afternoon there. The new married folks intending to lodge at her house in Old Meldrum, [they] leaves the bridegroom's father's for the latter place about five o'clock, it beginning now to darken and the storm increasing. I accompanied the party as far as the turnpike road where I took leave of them, turned homeward. The snow still falling thick with a brisk wind from East. I made home without difficulty by a little past seven evening.

3rd, February, 1823
This morning the storm is still increased and is very deep now. Wreaths are from four to six feet deep and has every appearance of a growing storm. Have ranked out a man with a cart and two horses to take home my wife from Old Meldrum, and from tempestuousness of the day looks to be a difficult work, the snow being deep and drifting terribly. He however set out and succeeded in bringing her home here a little after four o'clock. She intended coming by the Mail Coach Sunday evening, but there not being room had to stop all night, and it so happened that her sister, the new married wife, fell in labour during the night and bare a girl, which with the mother was in a fair way when she left that about midday.

15th March, 1823
My father tells me today that he intends marrying his housekeeper. The weather is now very fine . . .

24th March, 1823
Margaret is sent to school this day for first time.

13th April, 1823
Got ready this day about eleven o'clock and went up to my father's, who has got himself married before kirk time, about half past eleven, to a Jane Nicol, sister of Alexander Nicol, Burreldales. She has kept house for my father since Martinmas. He had no acquaintance of her before.

1st June, 1823
Went to church . . . When I came home found my wife ill. Had been ill and continued in extremity until about five o'clock when she bare a dead male child, the body of which was not so well formed as could have been wished. I immediately sent off the wrights to get a coffin made and to the grave digger to make a grave. Got my father and brother down and interred the child the same afternoon he was born. My wife is poorly, being terribly racked, but I think she has suffered no irreparable injury and expects she will soon get over.

10th June, 1823
The child Mary has begun to walk alone a little this day for the first time.

15th June, 1823
The children, Adam and Margaret, have been at kirk today. This is the first time to either of them.

24th June, 1823
At twelve went out to Cranna to the burial of Elspet Mackie, my father's sister.

10th September, 1823
. . . and man to the moss: took home two freights peats. Gave Thain, the schoolmaster, one freight, two loads, to be the children's school firing through the winter.

12th September, 1823
Wrote Thain this morning about the severity of the discipline to the boy Adam: said if he could not manage him with less flogging to send him home. His tardings will be distinct on his backside for a week or ten days.

3rd January, 1824
The third day of January ends another year of my life. I this day enter the thirty-seventh year of my age in health and in peace. My family also all well . . .

My family at the present time consists of one boy, Adam, and two girls, Margaret and Mary, all strong and healthy. Adam, born 7th May 1817, is now six years and eight month old . . . Mary, born 12th October, 1821, is now two years and three months old, is a fine healthy child running about speaking as much as to ask what she wants. The other two are at school, Adam since 18th March, 1822, Margaret since 24th March, 1823. [They] are both coming on tolerable. Adam has been reading in the New Testament and a collections the last nine or ten months. Margaret is put into the same about a month since.

My wife's present appearance an additional member to the family bespeaks, in the course of the present year. My servants during the winter half year, and who have continued with me since Whitsunday last, are James Singer, man; James Castel, boy; Bell Wallace and Helen Jameson, women servants.

15th January, 1824

We were this morning alarmed by the sudden and unexpected death of William Jameson, my wife's brother. He had been unwell for two or three weeks back and came out here from Old Meldrum Friday last to put off the time a little as he was off work and, I understood, to take the advice of our lodger, Dr Chalmers. The few days he was here he got himself twice blooded and once blistered and we thought he was getting better, as he appeared frank and lively for the most part. The doctor described his disorder to be inflammation of the lungs and an abscess having broke there was what he supposed proved so suddenly fatal. He went to bed after being at card playing until about two o'clock morning. He slept soundly (by the account of a person that was in the same apartment) until eight o'clock morning when he got up and came to the kitchen, which as he was entering [he] seemed to lay hold on the doorposts to support himself, when my own man and another person (who happened to be in the kitchen) flew to his assistance and brought him to a seat. The doctor and myself was immediately called (not being out of bed). He appeared to me as if in a fit and was making every effort to get breathed, which went out and in apparently by mere force, his countenance much distorted. He continued in this situation for near an hour when he breathed his last. I assisted at washing him, put a clean shirt on him, and had his body laid out. And as soon as that was settled sent my man away to Old Meldrum to give his friends notice.

So sudden an unexpected death cast a damp on my mind and I could not help being sad throughout the day. It is a comfort to me to think my wife is not alarmed to be the worse [sic]. He is the first person that I have seen die. I assisted in supporting him on a chair to the last. In consequence of a death happening in the house I resolved not opening my shop, but numbers of people calling disturbed the house so much that I considered it would be better to open, which I did.

16th January, 1824

This morning I got up early, about four o'clock, to relieve those that have been sitting up. Have attended my shop through the day. I still feel thoughtful on the brittleness of the thread of life. Perhaps the seeds of death are lurking in some secret corner of our body and ready to cut us off, for in the midst of life we are in death. My mind seems fully laid open to serious reflection. The uncertainty of life even for another hour hangs on my inmost thoughts. All worldly things seem to lose their value and sink into nothing. Why should we hunt at trifles in which we cannot promise ourselves another hour's indulgence? If God were at present to withdraw my life, I would be in a less composed state of mind than I remember to have hitherto been. I pray that God may give me grace so to act that I may be always ready to give up my soul when he shall be pleased to call for it. Search me, O God and try me and see if there be any allowed evil in me and lead me in the way everlasting.

17th January, 1824

This morning we are busily employed making preparations for the funeral of William Jameson. The folks were invited to meet at 10 o'clock and they came up about 12, took some refreshment, and were ready to lift at about half past one. The body was laid down about two. He was in the twenty first year of his age, and a thick lusty man. [He] is buried at the head of my mother's grave. Gave dinner to the deceased's Old Meldrum friends and had a very throng afternoon in the shop.

22nd February, 1824

Was at my brother's this after[noon], hearing his child baptised— called George after himself.

7th May, 1824

My wife has passed an uneasy night in a languid-like state. Have had little rest, any of us. She continues much the same this day up to the present time, one o'clock. Took dinner and went up to the roup of the late R. Henry, Woodhead. Came home about seven o'clock, an hour previous to which my wife had been delivered of a boy and all in an ordinary way.

9th May, 1824
Got myself in dress and went up to Mr Thain, schoolmaster, and got the child's name, William, in the session book . . . Had a few friends at dinner this day. My father and brother with their wives; Mr Rose and daughter; Mr Neil; and Dr Chalmers, our lodger. Minister called at about half past four and baptised the child. Company dismissed about seven. Wife I think continues in a fair way of recovery.

25th October, 1824
Evening in company for some time with Mr Neil and doctor [Chalmers]. All my folks at Mr Hay's Ball except James Singer, who with his sore leg is now able to stir very little from his bed. Am beginning to think it is a rose wrong managed. Our lodger Dr Chalmers attends him.

2nd November, 1824
My man, James Singer, thinks his leg a little better today, and has gone away in a cart to his mother's house at Saphock.

6th November, 1824
Bell Wallace, our servant lass, has taken in her bed today complaining on a sore throat.

7th November, 1824
Our younger daughter, Mary, taken ill since last night. Am afraid it is the scarlet fever and sore throat.

8th November, 1824
Our sick folks are yet no better. Bell Wallace is seriously ill with fever and sore throat. The child Mary continues languid, but as yet am not convinced whether it be the fever or not.

13th November, 1824
Bell Wallace, our servant maid, a little better. Has got out of bed a short time today. The girl Mary is also better.

14th November, 1824
James Singer, my man, who has been away with a sore leg, has come back tonight.

15th November, 1824
Our servant maid, Bell Wallace, has gone away today being a little better. Her aunt's man, Alex McKenzie, Gordounston, came for her with a cart.

18th November, 1824
Our servant maid, Cirsty Scattertie, is away today with a sore throat. We are too bare of servants now.

20th November, 1824
At Turriff feeing market today. Engaged Charles Main, man, at present with Alex Watson, Hadow, at £7. A son of James Buns, Petty, for boy—John Bun at £3.

3rd January, 1825
This day I complete the thirty-seventh year of my age—another sensible intimation that time is making no stops, and whether we improve it or not the present moment will not wait or give us leisure to think whether we have employed it aright or not . . . My family, which now consists of two sons and two daughters (the oldest Adam in his eighth year and the youngest William about 8 months), are all in good health and in the midst of plenty. I am contented and may well be so.

1st May, 1825
Our youngest child, William, who has been a little indisposed for a week back is got much worse today. He will take nothing but drink and that vomits up nearly as soon as taken. His thirst appears to be excessive. We are alarmed for him. He seems seriously ill. He is sufficiently open in the bowels also.

2nd May, 1825
Passed the forepart of last night in bed although not very sound rest. Was surprised at about three o'clock by my wife declaring that the

child was dying. I get up and called ben the doctor, who could not say whether it actually was the case or not. He proposed applying leeches to his temples, which had the effect of rousing him. He, the doctor, thinks the disorder is situated in the child's head. We have hitherto conjectured that it was his stomach wrong in consequence of teething. He is now about one year old . . . My wife and some neighbours has sat with the child steady. He is weak, drinks and throws again. Sleeps with his eyes partly open—the eyeballs moving from side to side.

3rd May, 1825

The child who is now taking the chief part of our attention I think is a little lightened this morning. He has been sat up with by Bell Rose and one of our own girls. Has passed the night much the same as the day yesterday. Drinking and vomiting, sleeping with his eyes open some unseemly-like, is so very weak at times that we was called up to see whether there was breath in him or not, about two o'clock. During the day he is extremely weak—has refused drink towards even. My wife says he is just dying, and from every appearance he cannot be expected to survive long. The doctor thinks his disease is situated principally in his head—thinks there is some tendency to water there.

4th May, 1825

Myself and my father's wife has sat up with the child this night. He has slept mostly or lain in some kind of faint or stupor resembling sleep, only that his eyes are rarely right shut. He is however during the day considered better and we have again a little hope that he will live.

5th May, 1825

The child's disorder continues a little lightened. He is able to sit up a little and is not near so much distressed as he was. Myself and one of the girls sat up with him. He passed the forepart of the night in apparent profound sleep.

6th May, 1825

The child has been sat up with this last night by Bell Rose and one of our own girls. He is much easier, but my wife is afraid to trust herself asleep with him.

7th May, 1825
The child continues to keep better. We took him to bed with ourselves last night making one of our own girls and George Mackie's lass, Jane Wallace, sit up with us for two hours or so.

3rd August, 1825
Was a little alarmed this afternoon by Mr John Ogilvie (excise officer, presently lodging here) falling into an apoplectic fit. He had not lain above two or three minutes when the noise of his fall caused me to be called in. I assisted him up. It was about a quarter of an hour after he was seated on a chair before he knew me or where he was.

6th August, 1825
Had Mr Neil and Mrs Ogilvie, our exciseman's wife, from Tarves paying him Mr O, a visit. They interrupted three or four hours of my time in the middle of the day.

9th October, 1825
Was up this afternoon at George Mackie's. His wife has born him a son, their second, early this morning. My wife was called at a little past twelve at night.

16th October, 1825
This afternoon was up at George Mackie's. He has got his child baptised today, named Adam.

3rd January, 1826
. . . and I do this day complete another year of my age. I am now 38 years. Myself and my family are all in good health at present. My two oldest children, Adam and Margaret, continues at school, are both reading in the Bible, and have begun writing six or eight months since. The next oldest, Mary, is sometimes set to say over the alphabet but cannot yet do it alone. The bustle of business and work here causes her to be neglected. The youngest child, William, although we had given up all hopes of his life in May last, is now strong and healthy. The present appearance of my wife bespeaks an increase of family very soon.

17th January, 1826

Last night a little after ten o'clock my wife thought herself unwell and that child-bed labour was coming on her. I accordingly sent both men away and the two horses. The storm being deep I feared them not getting forward and sent the two, that the one might take charge of the horses and the other proceed on foot. They however found no material obstruction and was here with the [mid]wife about half past twelve—Betty Scott, wife to James Cowie, Blindmills. After passing a weary night, my wife was delivered of a boy about five o'clock this morning. She was fully as ill with pains after delivery as she was before, which continued through the most of this day. Her confinement at this time was in our own bed closet, the room that we generally use for that purpose being occupied by Mr Taylor, hose merchant, and him in bed before she grew badly.

22nd January, 1826

This afternoon have got our child baptised and named him (George). Have had a few of our neighbours at dinner: say Mr Wilson and his sister; my father; brother; and George Carl junior, with their wives; also the two Miss Roses. Spent an agreeable afternoon and dismissed about eight o'clock.

29th April, 1826

My employment this day has been packing eggs. Adam and Margaret has lifted them in over the box, amongst the first times either of them has been of any use.

5th May, 1826

Our child William was taken suddenly ill in bed about ten o'clock with a rouping kind of cough and difficulty in breathing. We was considerably alarmed and thought he was dying. Called the doctor out of bed, who caused him be put into a warm bath for eight or ten minutes and applied a blister to his throat, the which application relieved him a little. We had little or no rest throughout the night

6th May, 1826

The child William we think a little better. He kept his bed all day and slept mostly. He was a healthy prattling child before he was attacked with this blast. He is about two years old. He had a severe illness when we thought him dying about one year back.

7th May, 1826
Had my sister Betty Mackie in from Turner Hall here paying us a visit. Our child William we think is a little better today.

11th May, 1826
When I came home I found that another of our young ones, Margaret, had fallen sickly which we feel is the same disorder William has had—he is now getting better.

12th May, 1826
Margaret is rather worse. Her trouble turns out to be scarlet fever and sore throat. She had got a vomit this afternoon, has got her throat washed with vinegar and honey and a blister applied to the outside.

13th May, 1826
Margaret still continues badly. Her skin is covered with red spots. I feel a little fatigued, as also my wife, not getting good rest during the night.

14th May, 1826
Helen Jameson, my wife's sister, has been taken ill with the fever this morning . . . Another of our children, Mary, has been taken ill with fever and sore throat this afternoon.

15th May, 1826
I feel myself not altogether well—a severe cold and soreness of bones. Was nearly done out before I get my preparations for travel finished. The child Mary has got a vomit this afternoon, the operation we thought would have killed her. As well as vomiting, she passed an unnatural quantity of matter from her bowels, and through the night so overpowered with sickness that we thought she should have died. The doctor was called up who applied leeches to her temples and kept bathing her head with warm water. We went to bed at one o'clock and Jane Robertson, who came on chance to pay us a visit, sat up the rest of the night.

16th May, 1826
The children been much the same today with the exception of Mary, who it appears has been much distressed with sickness. Have not been well at all myself, back and bones wearied and a heat on my skin. Miss Rose of the Toll Bar sat up all night with the children.

17th May, 1826
This morning we think the children a little easier, but which has not had duration. Mary is so very ill in the afternoon that I cannot help thinking that she can[not] live long. She is complaining much, her countenance changing colour—blue, red and white—and a tremulous motion in her head. I cannot help being alarmed.

18th May, 1826
I have sat up the bypast night with Mary until five o'clock. She has been in great distress throughout the night, but not so alarmingly ill as last afternoon. She has not slept perhaps above five minutes at a time. What vexes me is that we cannot discover where the seat of her principal complaint is. She says it is her throat, but there is no right symptom to warrant that being the case. The doctor describes it [as] a general uneasiness. She makes a sudden cry as [if] it were stitches and throws herself about in bed, has a severe cough which is followed by retching or an inclination to vomit. Her eyes when open keeps floating about (as it were) in her head . . . The child Mary has continued throughout the day in much the same condition she was through the bypast night—much racked with pain the fundamental cause of which we have not yet discovered. Margaret and Helen Jameson are recovering, the first was up for a few minutes this afternoon.

19th May, 1826
Mary appears a little easier this morning but has passed a restless night. Our lass, Mary Sinclair, sat with her and I relieved at 4 o'clock morning. The fever seems to set in regular. Her skin has begun to spot in the course of the day.

20th May, 1826
I little thought yesterday when I noted down what I considered to be the state of Mary's health or rather of her disease, that my very next would be the painful task of recording her death.

I had occasion to go to Turriff market this day as I wanted a man. I considered the child out of danger this morning as the disease had assumed a more regular appearance and on that account my mind was comparatively at rest. But how vain and ill founded does our most ardent expectations turn out. I had not arrived at my own house above half an hour when the child breathed her last. She had been much tossed through the afternoon and distressed with retching. When I came in she was tumbling and moaning and crying 'alas'. I asked what was worst of her, she said her throat, and called for a drink of ale, when she got a drink of water that was allotted for her drink.

Oh how painful to my feelings have been the sufferings of this little innocent, agonised to the last degree, yea even until death, and me an onlooker during her worst afflictions and could not afford her the smallest relief. Do thou, O God, sanctify unto us every dispensation of thy providence that we may see thy hand in all our sufferings and yield a cheerful obedience as we know thy judgements are unsearchable and thy ways past finding out.

21st May, 1826

This day we are comparatively at ease on the child's account. George Ironside brought a coffin by ten o'clock and she was laid in it. Her skin is getting blue. Her eyes (which in consequence of the agony of her death never closed right) are sunk in her head.

Have not been at church nor any of the family. In the afternoon had in a few women, our neighbours, at a cup of tea. The child was sat up with last night by Dr Chalmers, George Mackie, and Jane Robertson. Is to be sat with this night by two of George Mackie's shoemakers and my own boy, George Duncan. The rest of our folks are keeping pretty well in health as I think.

22nd May, 1826

This day we have done little or no work. Have had Mary's funeral this afternoon, which is the last service the little innocent will require of me. She was a stout healthy girl, rather more bashful in company than the rest of the children, but rambling enough among her equals, entirely free from guile or cunning. I trust her soul enjoys the bliss of heaven. She was born 12 October 1821, and at her death her age was four years seven months and eight days. Her grave in the churchyard is on the right side William Jameson with her feet at my mother's head.

24th May, 1826
Took up a few green feal with a cart and covered the child Mary's grave.

28th May, 1826
Our girl Margaret is recovering but slowly from the effects of her late fever.

31st May, 1826
The children Margaret and William are recovering but very slow from their late illness.

4th September, 1826
My wife has been unwell with a pain in her bowels. She has been unable to be out of bed.

5th September, 1826
My wife is as much recovered of her unwellness as that she has been able to keep shop.

14th September, 1826
Was also up at the school settling for the children's school fees for bygone year.

3rd January, 1827
This day I complete the thirty-ninth year of my age, being born 3rd January, 1788. Am in health and strength and have all my faculties in full vigour. My family also are all well, which at this time consists of a wife and four children, viz. Adam, Margaret, William and George . . .

Adam has been at school since March 1822, that is four years, ten months, is now reading in a collection of miscellaneous pieces and writing words of coarse big letters.

Margaret has been at school since March 1823, about three years and ten months. Her progress has been much the same as Adam's.

William is a fine little chatting child, but has several times been so much afflicted with ill health that his life has sometimes been despaired of.

George is a stout healthy roaring child. He unfortunately has a spot on his face on the centre of his forehead about the size of a sixpence and of the appearance of a rasp or a strawberry.

These are the members of our family at present but I do not see so far into futurity as can say that we shall all see the end of the year just begun. Our child, Mary, who died last May, was as healthy and as merry this time last year as any of us now are.

29th August, 1827

. . . making preparations for sending carts to Aberdeen—are letting them go a day sooner than usual on account of Adam and Margaret going with them to see the town etc. etc.

4th September, 1827

Sent man with a cart this afternoon to meet our little folks at Old Meldrum. They came by Inverurie Canal.

3rd January, 1828

This third day of January 1828, I complete the fortieth year of my age and am in good health and feel all my faculties unimpaired. My wife and children are also all in good health at present. Our family consists of the same members as did at this time last year.

Chapter 3

STUDY AND LEISURE

22nd August, 1819
I have been principally engaged this day studying at an *Encyclopaedia* by Nicholson, six octavo [volumes], a book sent by George Clark, Bookseller, Aberdeen. Invoiced at six guineas.

26th September, 1819
Am studying a part of the *Encyclopaedia Edinensis*, brought by a bookman, George Anton.

24th October, 1819
At home without company afternoon and evening, looking over a little of the *History of Aberdeen*, which I have got lately.

31st October, 1819
Had Mr Neil and Mr D. Rose at dinner and during the afternoon as also J.C. Rods, who came in by chance afternoon. The conversation tended little to the improvement of mind or regulation of life.

14th November, 1819
Afternoon reading some *History of the Devil*.

8th December, 1819
At even in company with Mr Scott from Aberdeen as also with some others in the house. Went to Singer's with Scott at night and came [home] late and went to bed.

9th December, 1819
I am uncommonly ill after last night's drink. Terrible sick and kept bed mostly.

12th December, 1819
Spent the evening reading *History of the Devil*, a shallow subject.

19th December, 1819
Afternoon and evening, reading Gifford's *History [of the] French Revolution*. The fate of Louis XVI sufficiently points out the instability of human greatness. In his first speech to his parliament, he says 'I am resolved to maintain my authority in all its plenitude. You are to learn to prize my favours and never lose the remembrance of their extent'. See him in 1790 accepting a new constitution that abolishes nobility and all hereditary offices and distinctions. In 1792, his authority is laid aside and royalty abolished. In 1793, he is taken to a scaffold and beheaded. Let him that standeth take heed lest he fall.

27th December, 1819
Went out forenoon with fishing rod attempting to take some salmon that were showing their heads in the Mary Pot. Did not succeed.

14th January, 1820
Little doing this day . . . Have been reading at Gifford's *History of the War* and have followed Bonaparte into Egypt in July 1798. That summer I was at Rothie keeping Mr Hay's cows and was ten years old.

25th January, 1820
In my shop doing little business there, and in the intervals reading Gifford's *History of the War*.

6th February, 1820
Have had no company this day with myself, and have gone on with my studies, tracing the courses of the French and British armies in Egypt in 1801.

17th February, 1820
Have been bad of a headache with last night's drink and disturbance.

26th March, 1820
Afternoon reading Rollin's *History*.

14th April, 1820
Have been little other than idle myself today. Went out a-fishing but had no success.

26th April, 1820
Went out a-fishing this forenoon. Took about a dozen.

30th April, 1820
Afternoon reading Rollin, wherein instruction may be learned. Indulge not in ease. It enfeebles the body and, although one could afford luxury, it should not be indulged. It enervates the whole mind and by imperceptible steps overcomes the whole frame.

14th May, 1820
Afternoon reading Rollin's history of Antiochus Epiphanus, who persecuted the Jews.

3rd September, 1820
Had George Carl in company this afternoon and the time spent with the domestic news of this neighbourhood.

2nd October, 1820
Held our winter at even. Had an agreeable company of neighbours. Dismissed about three next morning.

22nd October, 1820
Spent the evening reading Paulus Emillius's campaign in Macedonia and the overthrow of Perseus, the last king thereof.

3rd December, 1820
At even reading from Rollin the defeat of the Romans under Crassus, 54 BC., the history of Hieron, the good king of Syracuse, and the siege of Syracuse by the Romans under Marcellus, when it was reduced by them.

24th December, 1820
At kirk as usual. Spent the rest of the day and evening reading Addison's *Evidences of the Christian Religion.*

21st October, 1821
Have amused myself this evening reading the *Life of Christ.*

16th November, 1821
A dinner party here by Mr Neil our lodger. The company consisted of one supervisor, three officers of excise, one farmer, two merchants and one butcher. We parted about eleven o'clock. The Fyvie harvest ball is also this evening—two maids and little man at it.

2nd December, 1821
Filled up the rest of the time reading the *Life of Christ*, a work that suggests good ideas.

9th December, 1821
Was some little time up at my father's this afternoon. Afterwards reading Fleetwood's *Life of Christ*, an engaging discourse although not handled in my opinion to the same advantage it might have been.

16th December, 1821
Spent the evening reading Fleetwood's *Lives of the Apostles.*

25th August, 1822
Had some company this afternoon at dinner: say Mr Rait and wife; George Mackie and wife; Mr Rose and daughter; Mrs Milne; and Alan Robb from East Side, Newtoun of Auchterless, at whose house I commonly halt and take some dinner when travelling in

Auchterless. Spent a social afternoon and parted about half past seven o'clock.

29th August, 1822
Was up at dinner with Mr Thain, schoolmaster, which is a treat that I could have been happy to dispense with, but this being the fourth pressing invitation from him I was under the necessity of accepting it, that as it is necessary to keep the boy at the school I must try to keep in terms with the master—who is an inconstant kind of character, overbearing with his friendship, and a malicious reviler when his favour is lost.

21st November, 1822
Having an invitation to go up to Mr Thain's in the evening to make us acquainted with his new wife (as I suppose), my wife went up at six and I followed at nine and continued there till twelve. This treat I did not enjoy much. He is a person whose manner I don't like—is of a variable kind of temper.

8th December, 1822
Have employed this evening reading the history and theory of the gas lights from a number of an *Encyclopaedia*.

18th December, 1822
Bailey More from Old Meldrum with some books—put off some time in the forenight with him. Bought the *Spectator*, Harvey's *Meditations*, and *Arabian Nights*, all at 22/-.

11th May, 1823
This afternoon have had my father and his new wife at dinner with us.

27th July, 1823
Had company this morning as soon as I was in dress—Alex Robb, Newton, Auchterless, whom I had invited as I had some more folks coming in. I commonly dine with him when I am out collecting butter in Auchterless . . . Had company at dinner this afternoon: Mr Thain and wife; George Ironside and wife; James Duguid and wife; also Mrs Milne and the two Misses Rose; Mr Neil; Alex Robb; and Dr Chalmers. Spent the afternoon drinking toddy and dismissed between eight and nine at night.

28th September, 1823
Had no company. Passed the afternoon reading part of Boston's
Fourfold State.

28th December, 1823
In the evening had two pressing invitations to go up to Mr Thain's
to tea. I complied with the last and went up (my wife being there
before) and spent the evening.

26th January, 1824
Have been employed the forepart of this day writing a letter to
negotiate the purchase of an *Encyclopaedia Britannica* offered for
sale by George Clark, Aberdeen.

31st January, 1824
Have been in treaty for the purchase of an *Encyclopaedia Britannica*.
Caused Alexander Milne offer £12, but is not accepted, he, George
Clark, being insisting on £14 without 6d abatement. I must think
again before I offer so much.

6th February, 1824
Have been in the shop steadily this day (which has been cold and
blowing), reading in Hume's *History of England*—the Norman
Conquest.

26th June, 1824
Alex Milne advises of him having bought for me the *Encyclopaedia
Britannica*, 6th edition, the newest, at £21.

10th July, 1824
Have at this time got home the *Encyclopaedia Britannica* bought
by Alex Milne, Gallowgate, at £21 sterling Have been looking out
for a book of this kind for some time past. This copy (in board) is
considered cheap, the publisher's price being £36 sterling.

2nd November, 1824
Am in shop about steady this day doing little but reading Hume's
England.

23rd October, 1825
Was up at Mr Thain's in the evening. My wife had been up calling on her sister and was invited into Mr Thain's and I was then sent for.

7th January, 1826
Gave a kind of formal dinner this day to my servants and George Mackie's shoemakers etc. My own man, Charles Mair, so much debauched that he could not attend. These holidays does them much hurt as they are mostly drunk all the time.

9th October, 1826
Was in company in the evening with Mr Rait, grieve, Fyvie, and Peter Milne, Little Gight. They made themselves both groggy before they parted.

29th November, 1826
Was in company sometime in the evening with John Thomson, grieve at St John's Wells, and Mr A. Milne, Peterwell. Was all well to live by the time we parted.

18th December, 1826
Reading astronomy at even.

26th December, 1826
Went up myself to Woodhead to a dinner given to a few folks by Mr Emslie, gauger. Stopped there during the evening and came home about eleven o'clock. Drunk enough.

27th December, 1826
Have been much out of order this day in consequence of my last night's debauch. It was mid day before I was fit for shop-keeping.

12th January, 1827
Was engaged this forenoon sorting some lint yarn, and all the rest of my spare time reading *[Guy] Mannering*.

15th January, 1827
I have been in the shop all day and during the intervals of business
reading Scott's novel of *Redgauntlet.*

26th January, 1827
I continue in shop: am occupying my spare time reading Scott's
novel of *The Abbot.* The subject is chiefly on the manner of Queen
Mary's imprisonment in the Castle of Loch Leven, with her escape
from that imprisonment and from Scotland.

29th January, 1827
I have been engaged this day posting my shop books etc. : during
my spare time reading a novel—*The Pirate.*

5th February, 1827
Attending in shop and contriving some outdoor work, the weather
being fair and fine, and during my spare time reading *Waverley.*

16th February, 1827
Reading Scott's *Tales of my Landlord.* Consists of the prosecutions
and slaughters by the military [of] Covenanters in Charles 2nd's
time. Scene of the story lies in the County of Lanark.

15th July, 1827
Went out a little with my wife to a walk. Was joined by Mr and Mrs
Thain, who returned and took tea with us, and in this trifling manner
I spent the afternoon.

7th October, 1827
Employed myself reading Constable's *Miscellany*—voyages, muti-
nies, and shipwrecks in the Southern Ocean.

15th December, 1827
James Gall called on me at night, from whom I bought some
books: say Glasgow Geography, part of *Oxford Encyclopaedia*, and
Brown's Bible.

Chapter 4

RELIGION:
SERMONS AND REFLECTIONS

12th November, 1820

Have been at kirk today. Sermon from 21 Verse, 2 Chapter, Philippians: 'For all seek their own and not the things of Jesus Christ'. The subject went on the great selfishness of people and their wonderful attachment to the things of this world in preference to those of more importance—the things that belong to Jesus Christ. The inconstancy of men's conduct in this particular, who live and act as if born to themselves and for the gratification of the sensual and short lived pleasures of this world. The revolutions of states and the overthrow of kingdoms are the most momentous things of this world, which often affect the lives and property of millions, but all this put together is not worthy to be compared to the salvation of a single soul. Hence is the vast more importance of the Gospel preached to men above the deliberations of senates and the resolutions of parliaments. O that men would be wise that they would consider this before they are forever hid from their eyes. You that are young, offer unto God the spring of your life, the morning of your days: then shall you reap pleasant fruit in your old age and enjoy happiness for ever. You that are middle aged, suffer not the business of this world to engross all your attention. This life is a state of trial only, and but a moment in respect of that which is to come. You that are of age, remember now that you have not long to live and how wretched and unseemly even in this world is the old man who hath nothing but his age to make him respectable—dreadful thought: that men, until they are in sight of the grave, continue to indulge in the crimes and follies of this world without taking any thought of their never-dying souls. If there is any of this description before me now, I beg of you to turn

unto the Lord, who will have mercy on you, and unto our God, who
will abundantly pardon. This subject drew the audience's attention.

3rd January, 1821

As to religion, I am firmly persuaded of a future state of rewards
and punishments and that the enjoyment of the blessed state is
altogether beyond the power of man to conceive. May we therefore
satisfy ourselves to praise God for his goodness, who continues the
great blessing of health, that relish of all other enjoyments here, and
who hath appointed our lot in an enlightened country, where the
ordinances of religion are regularly dispensed. Grant, O God, that
we so spend our time here as we shall wish to have done when we
come to die.

29th April, 1821

At kirk as usual. Text, 32 Chapter, Isaiah, 15 Verse: 'Until the Spirit
be poured on us from on high'. An excellent sermon on the power
and influence of the Spirit of God, which like drops of fortifying rain
is more abundant at some times and in some places than other, as
was the case on the day of Pentecost. He seems to be convinced that
the time is approaching when in this world we shall live in harmony
together. It is incredible and almost beyond calculation the numbers
that meet death by the sword and other instruments of destruction
from the ambition of men bearing titles and invested with authority
amongst their fellow men, but it shall not be so when the Spirit
is poured out for the fruits of the Spirit are Love, Joy, Peace etc.
The nations shall not learn the arts of war any more, but they shall
beat their swords into ploughshares etc. It may not be our lot to see
those happy times in our day, but like David, who willingly laid in
materials for the Temple that he was never to see built, may we lay
up in store a stock of good deeds and virtuous actions that by precept
and example we may fit ourselves and posterity for the promised
happy times when the Spirit shall be poured from on high.

12th August, 1821

This our Communion Sabbath . . . Forenoon sermon by our own
minister from Isaiah, 53 Chapter, 2 Verse: 'For he shall grow up etc.
etc.' An excellent discourse for the present occasion. The mission of
our Saviour and reason for his low and humble appearance among

men explained: that if he had come in regal pomp he would only have been accessible to few and that the better sort, which was not the design of his ministry, and would have led them further into their error of expecting of him a temporal prince. If he had come in the Glory of his Divine Majesty, no human eye could have beheld him and lived, so that before we be able to behold the Glory of God, we must have new and stronger faculties. The very angels are unable to look on the full effulgence of the Face of God, and is represented by Isaiah as veiling their faces with their wings to hide them from the exceeding splendour of the Countenance of God. Such was the Love of God to men that he took on him the form of a servant, the character best suited to the capacities of mortal men, thereby giving us an example of love and humility that can never be imitated.

The rest of the service was gone through in the ordinary way. Mr Smith of Bourtie assisted, and preached in the afternoon from the 6 Chapter Ephesians, 1 Verse, 'that ye walk worthy of the vocation wherewith ye are called', useful exhortations that we persevere in the work of religion and holy lives, a[s] we are soon again to go out into the world and be exposed to temptations if we do not keep in mind the vocation wherewith we are called.

14th October, 1821
At church. Text, Acts, 26 Chapter, 18 Verse: 'To open their eyes and turn them from darkness to light etc., etc.' The necessary qualifications we must have before we can be meet for the society of Heaven, were it possible that we were to be admitted there and all our crimes about us, it would be no place of happiness. Let me ask the impious and profane what company they would join. The Prophets and Apostles would fly from you, the pure Angels would avoid you as a noxious thing, and your situation would certainly be truly unhappy unless you had been before prepared to join in the prayers and praises of the Redeemer and take part in the glorious harmony of Heaven. Now unto him that is able to keep you from falling and to present you faultless before his presence with exceeding joy, to the only wise God and our Saviour be eternal Glory and Praise, Amen.

2nd December, 1821
Was at church. Text, Romans, 4 Chapter, 7 and 8 Verses: [7]'Blessed are they whose iniquities are forgiven and whose sins are covered.

8. Blessed is the man to whom the Lord doth not impute sin'. He (the Minister) from time to time is admonishing us to come out from the world and to enter on the blessedness of God in Christ. Confesses he is unable to describe rightly what sin is. Scripture calls it the transgression of the Law, but we must all know that the least degree of it is of dreadful malignity. How trifling was the sin of Adam, who has plunged all his posterity in irreparable woes. Sin was the cause of the destruction of the old world and of Sodom and Gomorrah. What numberless wars and devastations hath sin brought on mankind and all this is but a faint idea of what sin is. Sin made Angels Devils and created Hell. Sin makes men associates with Devils and prepares inhabitants for Hell. But as in man all died, so in Christ shall all be made alive, if they will only embrace Him and live agreeable to His doctrine, and thereby accept the kingdom he hath prepared for them, the happiness of whose blessed state is beyond all conception. May each and all of us not only avoid sin, but live righteously that we may inherit the blessedness of those to whom the Lord will not impute Sin.

17th March, 1822

Have been at church today. Text, Genesis 7 Chapter, 21 Verse: 'And all flesh died that moved upon the earth, both of fowl and of cattle and of beast, and of every creeping creature that creepeth upon the earth, and every man'. The people of the old world we have reason to believe were far gone in wickedness and abounded in all sorts of vice. Noah was appointed to preach to them repentance and to prepare an ark for the safety of himself and family. But [neither] the word nor works of Noah had no [sic] effect on the hardened generation, and they only laughed and made sport of him for his instruction calling him a fool or a madman. May not the present age be compared to that in which the ark was built? Doth not the world at present lie in wickedness? Are not holy men slighted and ridiculed as fanatics, fools or mad men as Noah was? And what will be the dreadful end of all these things? What dreadful howling and shrieks at the destruction of the old world when people flocked in crowds to the highest hills, mountains and trees for safety and seeing their brethren swept off in droves and not the least ray of hope left for themselves. What bitter remorse of conscience that they did not attend to the wise admonitions of righteous Noah, whom they saw now floating in safety on the surface of the great ocean. May God

Almighty work in us holy desires that we be made worthy and enjoy his presence in Heaven for evermore. Amen.

24th March, 1822

I waited [for the] sermon there [at Auchterless]. Mr Dingwall lectured . . . The discourse in my opinion was rather destroyed than improved by the minister's thundering manner of delivery, the smallness of the church considered.

10th November, 1822

Heard a good sermon, as I conceived it, from 1 Peter, 5 Chapter and 5 Verse: 'Be clothed with Humility'. 'Humility', he says, is the best defence and ornament of the soul. To be humble is the road to honour and preferment, but humility does not consist in mean actions, coarse apparel, in associating with people of inferior rank. Humility is the thinking moderately of oneself and giving the preferment to others and the glory to God, who does not disdain the meanest object of the Creation. We may reasonably suppose that we are the lowest in the rational Creation, little originally and less by our fallen condition. Yet we are not overlooked in the immensity of God's works, who hath set an example of love and humility that can never be equalled in the death and suffering of Jesus. May God fill our minds with right notions of his infinite goodness and fix in our souls a love of holiness and a steadfast hope of Heaven. His [the minister's] subjects are generally well ordered and every Sunday I expect as it were an intellectual treat of which I am seldom disappointed, and at the time I feel my soul refreshed.

3rd January, 1823

That my children, who are yet young, are healthy, their intellects are sound and seem well formed, their bodies are right proportioned, [they] have the use of all their limbs and a perfect faculty of speech. For all these and numberless other mercies I bless God and pray that, since I am so abundantly provided for in this life, that he will not leave me destitute of qualifications suitable for the next, nor suffer me to so far forget myself as allow the business or transient pleasures in this life to interrupt me in making preparations for the next.

3rd January, 1824

During the jars of foreign states, we (in Scotland) have peace, and have had during my time. Our persons, property, and religion are secure, and in this land of liberty every man can worship God as his own conscience directs. The established church and minister is provided for the public gratis. Such privileges gives us an opportunity of being good men and good Christians, but these privileges, now grown common, are not esteemed as their importance deserve. Religion with many of us is but a secondary consideration, contenting ourselves with the surface of sacred things. To delineate the Deity methodically is perhaps what few have attempted and none accomplished, for we have not seen God at any time. Yet traces of his divine agency everywhere appear, opening a boundless field in the works of Creation and Providence for the contemplation of man, [so] that the utmost stretch of his imagination can only form a confused idea, losing himself in wonder and amazement at such infinite greatness, forcing as it were on his mind a sense of the wisdom and goodness of his Creator, [so] that though he cannot comprehend he can admire and adore.

I confess I have received liberally of the mercies of God. His bounty hath made my cup to run over, in difficulties and dangers [I] have been led in a way I thought not of.

Now I pray God, who hath abundantly provided for me throughout life, may make this day to me the birth day of my soul, born again by the regenerating influence of Grace through Jesus Christ, that while diligent in business I may be fervent in spirit, preserving a correspondence with Heaven that I may so establish myself and my family in the graces of that happy place that we may dwell with God and good men for ever.

18th January, 1824

This morning proceeded in my ordinary course of catechising the children and then went to church.

3rd January, 1825

In my family I have contentment and in my neighbourhood [I] am respected. I have good bodily health which sweetens every other enjoyment, and I may say my lot has fallen in pleasant places, and it is my duty to give God the glory who hath led me in such green pastures. May thou therefore, my Almighty Creator, be pleased to accept my sincere acknowledgments of all thy mercies, and may I always live grateful to the power that supports me in existence and that has preserved me from danger and great difficulties. Be pleased, O God, to continue thy mercies and may I in all my doings and dealings keep in mind that Thine all-seeing eye is upon me. May my young ones be brought up in thy fear and favour and be preserved from the follies that childhood and youth are subject to. May each of us spend our time in such a manner as that whatever we do it may be to the glory of God, that our life and conduct be such as shall be approved by thee at last. That this be our happy lot do thou O God of thy mercy grant.

27th November, 1825

At church this day. Text, Ecclesiastes, 9 Chapter, 10 Verse: 'Whatsoever thy hand findeth to do, do it with all thy might'. The duty of industry explained and enforced by argument on the benefit of exercise; that labour is necessary to many and laudable and healthy to all; that those who are set above the need of manual labour owes a duty to society and themselves of not being uselessly indolent; that the man who does his part of manual labour is more useful to the public than the rich man who does nothing. That although the unconnectedness of the subject with religion appears out of place from the pulpit, yet it may be admitted on the score of harmonizing society in recommending habits of honest industry as a preparatory to that more blessed society in Heaven to which we all aspire, and may our conduct now be such as shall be no bar at last to our entrance to that happy place.

3rd January, 1826

For the last eight or ten years we have had national peace both at home and abroad and at this present time there is peace and plenty over the land, and in our particular district we have all the comforts that the country affords, and enjoys the same free from molestation. For my own part, if I make exception of a little confinement which the nature of my business requires, I have every other indulgence in my situation that money can bring. But such is the depravity of man's nature that he is least grateful when he has most favours. The good things of this world blinds our eyes and takes hold of our hearts, [so] that we are ever ready to forget the hand wherewith they are bestowed, so inconsistent is man if he is not granted grace

along with his other good things. Be pleased therefore, O thou great
first cause and absolute dispenser of all things to instil into our souls
the emanations of thy grace that in all our doings and dealings we
may have God always before us. May we ever keep in mind that
we are accountable creatures and that this life is only our progress
to another more blessed and everlasting, and that, having finished
our course and kept the faith, we may at last sit down with God,
the Father, Son and Holy Spirit, and all the glorious company in
Heaven.

12th February, 1826
Have been at church. Mr John Stott preached . . . His discourse
was a good one but rather more dry and formal than what we are
accustomed to from our own minister.

15th October, 1826
Was at church. Mr Dingwall of Auchterless preached . . . made a
good discourse, but what makes him not altogether [pleasing] to us
is his roaring manner of delivery.

3rd January, 1827
As to the business of religion, I may safely say that as a country,
family, or individuals we have not made that progress which the
importance of the subject deserves, and how this is to be accounted
for I cannot comprehend. We see almost every person anxious to
procure a comfortable situation here and why he is not more earnest
to secure a comfortable and happy situation in the world to come is
something to be wondered at in a self interested set. Is it because
he imagines that state far off? Or is it because he is not absolutely
certain of a future state of rewards and punishments? Or what is
it that damps his ardour in his pursuit of his interest in the most
important of all concerns?. I may leave off the subject. I cannot
solve it. The whole creation we see contributes to our comfort and
happiness. Our own bodies and everything in nature is wonderful
and wisely formed and we are the most ungrateful of all beings that
can be imagined if we do not reverence and adore the cause of all
our comforts, and have our whole life and conversation regulated
agreeable to the perfect pattern of holiness and virtue set before us in
the Gospel, adoring God and our Lord and Saviour Jesus Christ that
we may be found worthy and qualified at last for entering into the

happiness of Heaven when God shall be pleased to withdraw us from thence, and to his Great and Glorious Name be for ever praise.

11th February, 1827
At church. Text, Genesis, 41 Chapter, 38 Verse: 'And Pharaoh said unto his servants—Can we find such a one as this is, a man in whom the spirit of God is'. A good discourse on the purity of Joseph's principles and so worthy of imitation. There was much coughing amongst the congregation, which irritated the minister [so] much that he said he would better sit down or they had done, which when he did [and] all was quiet, he got up again and said it seemed it was only to give disturbance that such coughing was indulged, as they could hold when they thought proper. They surely were instigated by the Devil to use such freedoms.

10th June, 1827
At church. Two sermons given for first time this season, and both without interval. A new method, this the first trial, intended to keep people from going home between the sermons. The first discourse was a lecture on 62 Psalm: 'Truly my soul waiteth upon God etc.' The second was a sermon from Ephesians, 5 Chapter, 8 Verse: 'For ye were sometimes darkness, but now ye are light in the Lord walk as children of light'. A fine discourse on the excellence of Religion, its importance and happy consolations in the end. May our conduct be always conformable to our professions.

3rd January, 1828
While other countries are visited with war and bloodshed, we in Scotland have peace and plenty and most of the comforts and conveniences of life which advantages might reasonably be expected to make us good men and good Christians. The present season also bring a fresh admonition that another of those years that mark the progress of our time has revolved, silently insinuating you have one year less to live and tacitly asks the question: 'has the bygone year added much to your stock of wisdom, knowledge and virtue? Is your soul established in righteousness and qualified for meeting with God? If not now, when will it be? What certainty had you last year at this season that you should be alive until now?' These are questions which I stand in awe of in answering, for I find that except through the atonement of a Redeemer I shall never be perfect before

God. It is not in man of himself so much as to think a good thought, but on the mercy of God we must rely for all things. His goodness at first called us into being and has sustained us to the present moment, has made our lot to fall in pleasant places in an enlightened civilized and Christian country where every man can worship God as his conscience directs. I will bless the Lord with my soul and all that is within me be stirred up to bless his holy name. Now, O God, as thou hast provided for us abundantly here be pleased to give us grace of thee to be fitted and prepared for giving up our account at last that we be admitted into the happiness of Heaven for evermore.

PART II

BUSINESS MATTERS

3. Where Adam went to market. Turriff

Chapter 5

SHOPKEEPER, INNKEEPER
AND MERCHANT

7th July, 1819
St Sair's Fair . . . At even attending the market folks with corn and grass for their horses—and as usual finds the Buchan people scruples and unwilling to pay for their horses.

13th July, 1819
Two [excise] general supervisors here. Went round and ranged Gordonstoun. Did not survey any here nor in this neighbourhood.

15th July, 1819
Arranging shop goods, making paper bags . . . , making up goods for taking to Auchterless.

18th July, 1819
Beginning an alphabetical catalogue of shop goods. A clear afternoon.

21st July, 1819
Packing eggs, attending shop. This the hose merchant's day.

19th August, 1819
In the morning had some company with carriage and horses going from Leith Hall to Carnies in Buchan. Had to attend them.

21st August, 1819

In the morning employed at my shop books. In the forenoon weighing and sorting butter casks. Received accounts that the butter was duller in sale. My own carts arrive at six afternoon from Aberdeen, being in with the first lot butter I have offered for sale this season. William Davidson, who hath been the principal buyer and to whom it was sent, says he has no orders at present and others are much of the same mind. The heat is so great that it has a great chance of wasting and they further excuse themselves by saying the Aberdeen price, 84/-, is too near the London price, 90/-, and will not afford any profit, which no doubt is the case. This butter trade is always fluctuating and the present reverse at this season gives a damp to my expectations, with 105 casks, about seven tons, on hand.

23rd September, 1819

Making up goods for the morrow's sale in Auchterless.

24th September, 1819

At Auchterless collecting butter.

11th October, 1819

Mostly engaged making preparations for Forgue. A rainy day mostly throughout. At night in company with Thomas Ogilvie and his brother. Bought from them thirty-eight yards Hodden at 11 pence and 146 yards Osnaburg at 4½ pence.

18th November, 1819

In my shop for most part. Called on Dr Argo for settlement of account or a bill. Did not succeed.

7th December, 1819

This day I have employed myself dipping candle. Have done about three stone. Are middling well made and the first I ever tried myself.

17th January, 1820

This morning was at my father's at breakfast. Spent the morning with Petty that was over settling an account. Bartered watches with him. Little more but eating and drinking going on.

12th January, 1820
This day have been mostly in the house forenoon.

13th January, 1820
Have kept shop this day and been posting books.

15th January, 1820
This morning I have received a box of tea from London by the Turriff carriers. I had invoice and advice 4 January that it was shipped 29 December. I did not insure which made me sometimes a little uneasy having also at sea fourteen casks butter and one cask snuff—about £12 sterling value—coming from Glasgow, altogether about £90 value. Have no advice of butter being arrived at Leith or snuff at Aberdeen.

27th January, 1820
Salting one cask butter this day. Called on Dr Argo to speak about the settlement of his account or to give a bill for it. Making preparations for Aberdeen, intending to set out at night.

1st February, 1820
Continued arranging goods. Went to Dr Argo and took his bill for his account at three months. At even entering invoices.

3rd February, 1820
Have a cask snuff this day from Glasgow, with 7/7 charge thereon.

12th February, 1820
Mostly employed with shop business today . . . Have received advice this day of Adam Cruickshank, Turriff, carriers cart being robbed at night on the street at Aberdeen and a chest of tea from Thomas Young, London, to me is taken away. The cart by other accounts was not in street but in locked court.

16th February, 1820
Fastern's-even market this day is custom free for the first time. Constables get dinner here today by the laird's orders. We have had

a good market—taken about £12 house, £6 shop, and £4 stables. The day and the ground was dry and all passed over without anything remarkable.

17th February, 1820
This day have done nothing beyond shop business . . . Have got notice of the tea being found that was robbed from the carrier's cart between the tenth and eleventh inst. and the rogues lodged in jail.

12th March, 1820
Received advice this day from Leith of twenty cask butter being sold at 72/-, 74/-, and 76/-

11th April, 1820
Forepart of this day hiding whisky for fear of general supervisors that are in the country doing much mischief. One anker Miss Hay's dyke, one in peat stack, half ditto in the stones between the lime shade and the water.

20th April, 1820
Busy through the day with clover seed customers. Rye grass in demand is very scarce here, being frosted forepart of last summer—lowest price is 3/- and highest I ever heard of is 5/- the bushel of twenty lbs Dutch.

29th April, 1820
Alex Fraser, painter, left this place this morning without settling with me, but gave Mr Rose, Toll Bar, two pounds to pay me. I sent for William Urquhart and detained his trunk.

24th May, 1820
Jane Pratt ran away this morning, who I had engaged for summer lass and had been here three or four days. She has been in the same practice before and so continues.

17th June, 1820
Correcting yesterday's accounts, occasionally assisting wright who is putting doors on new houses. Had a busy day in shop. Mr Hay called for his account.

21st July, 1820
Gauger called at night. Paid him malt duty £2.2, ale licence £2.2, and 16/- tea and tobacco licence.

9th August, 1820
This Lammas Fair, Turriff . . . About four south dealers here at breakfast, but none throughout the night . . . Have this day solicited payment of the doctor's bill, or a renewal with a cautioner. He proposes his father.

19th August, 1820
Wrote out Dr Argo's bill for £22.18.6 and sent up for signature.

23rd August, 1820
In shop the most part of this day. Hose merchant here—a little busier than ordinary with his wives.

1st September, 1820
This Bartle Fair's day went to market in company with Alexander Robb of Newton who had a cow here the preceding night after being some time in market. Bought her at £5.10/-. Also in market bought a branded one year old quey at £3.5/-. Cattle are rather lower in price than they have been through the summer. In consequence the market is dull, holders not wishing to submit to the fall. Cheese is 6/- to 6/6 and 7/-. Few in it, not above half the usual quantity. Man home from Aberdeen. Butter 68/-, eggs 6 pence, meal is expected further down on account of British ports being opened for importation of foreign grain for three months from Lammas, the last quarter's price being something above the import price.

2nd September, 1820
Called on Dr Argo this evening and got the renewed bill on his account from him, with his own name and his father's at it.

12th September, 1820
Sold George Morison, Gordonstoun, one boll bear at 24/-, for which I take six pints whisky that being the same at 4/-, that article having got up 1/- since about three weeks back. Also bought from Charles Meldrum fourteen pints of what he calls Highland whisky

at 4/-, which is a better bargain than the low country whisky at same money.

28th September, 1820
Employed packing eggs. Had company of gentlemen at dinner from the funeral of Mrs Rose, relict of the late minister of Auchterless. The company consisted of a Provost More and Mr James Dyce from Aberdeen; Mr Hay, Rothie; Mr Irvine, Towie; Mr James Barclay, Auchterless; the ministers of Auchterless and Fyvie; Mr Cowie, schoolmaster, Auchterless, and his son; and Mr Murray, Newmill. Made ready orders and sent a cart to Aberdeen.

4th October, 1820
Continue doing a little at shop books this morning. Begun a calculating the measure and weight of oil. Put off some time at that and cannot render it right satisfactory after all . . .

16th October, 1820
Wholly employed this day in sorting by goods in shop and taking in a half puncheon of molasses and a five hundredweight cask of oil.

17th October, 1820
Have been employed this day removing the whiteiron pipes that filled the big spirit cask. Found them quite rotten, have taken down the wall, replaced them with lead pipes and built up the same again.

1st November, 1820
In the intervals of this day's business have been employed hiding whisky and making some preparations for my Auchterless journey on Friday. Intending to go to Turriff market tomorrow to buy a horse.

27th November, 1820
Have been employed enlarging a shelf this day in order to make room for some piggery that I cannot get rightly stowed.

14th December, 1820
This morning set a watch which succeeded in catching the boy, John Mackie, pilfering from the pantry the cash collected in the house.

For some time back he has been observed overfull of cash and last Sunday morning [there] was taken from the house till 11/- or 12/-. A slight suspicion fell on him, who confirmed it on himself the Tuesday following by slipping out three shillings. When found by Gammie and myself with the till in his hand he confessed after some interrogation that he had abstracted therefrom £4.10. I took from him £1.17 that he had by him and some new bought books and dismissed him.

27th December, 1820
Put aside one anker Highland whisky that I took home last night. Bought from Charles Meldrum at £3.10.

Called on Dr Argo for payment of his bill. He puts me off to the month of February.

6th January, 1821
Had Mr Watt, one of excise rangers, wishing me to buy whisky at £8 sterling the anker. I will perhaps be under the necessity of taking one.

2nd March, 1821
Called down Dr Argo, who says he will pay part of bill and renew it this day week.

7th March, 1821
This the market day and has been astonishingly fine in the heart of ill weather. We have had an ordinary good market. House has drawn about £7, shop about £7, stables £1.14/-. Constables had dinner here by the laird's order and expense. The whole passed over without any extra disturbance here.

9th March, 1821
Partly in the house this day and partly replacing things removed previous to the market.

28th March, 1821
This day has been employed drawing on paper a dial plate for an intended kitchen clock.

31st March, 1821
Was in company some time this morning with Chas. Craig and a whisky smuggler. Alex Singer joined. Went out with him to a roup of wood at Fyvie. Spent some time at Gardeners. Had Grant at even and some of his hunters drinking. £1 given them by Lord Huntly.

7th April, 1821
Have been preparing some boards for enclosing a [clock] movement intended for kitchen.

11th April, 1821
This the Turriff March market. Cattle are said to be a dull sale. Hose merchant here today. Have been engaged a little this afternoon putting up a kitchen clock.

12th April, 1821
Have been engaged the forepart of this day with Johnston Skene closing up the newly erected kitchen clock.

7th June, 1821
A burial from Aberdeen here this day—the late William Urquhart, Parkburn. Have had to assist to make preparations for dinner and accommodations for from twenty to thirty people. Also out meeting the same. Auchterless goods made up afterwards.

4th September, 1821
Made a new jotter book. Some carriages here today passing with company to Dunlugas.

10th September, 1821
Have had Gardener, gauger, and some others in the house drinking and making noise all day.

26th September, 1821
Measuring out and filling some cags and jars oil for taking out to Forgue. Doing sundries in shop. Trying to kill rats in the cart shade—they are very thick there.

27th September, 1821
Settled with Mr Neil for eleven weeks keep and lodgings to himself and shalt at 12/- a week them both.

27th October, 1821
Neil seized and brought in seven ankers whisky at night.

6th December, 1821
Have been packing eggs today, about 150 dozen, assisted loading carts and making out Aberdeen orders . . . Brought home meal from the mill, twelve and a half bolls . . . [Carts] set out for Aberdeen about eleven at night.

7th December, 1821
Attended shop and made ready casks for putting meal in.

8th December, 1821
In shop mostly, arranged casks and boxes in a long shade. Prepared some ankers to hold whisky that I expect on Monday . . . Carts home from Aberdeen about eight at even, heavy loaded.

21st December, 1821
Men threshing bear. Gave the straw to the doctor, he being short of thatch to his house.

25th December, 1821
Men have been in barn threshing out some bear. Have winnowed up three bolls. One sold to Adam Hay and one to gardener, Rothie, each at eight pints whisky a boll. I calculate the whisky at half a crown the pint and the best price for bear is twenty shillings.

3rd January, 1822
I have been very constant kept in my shop today, and also I have run out of a number of general articles, more than I ever remember of being short of at one time, say: sugar, tobacco, snuff, oil, candles, and salt. But I have wrought on as well as I could with the goods I have and gave fair words for the rest. I have taken in about an anker and a half of whisky from my outhouse cask.

18th January, 1822
Bruce, supervisor, here. Spent some time with him and Neil. Neil home drunk at night and made some outcast about his pony.

31st January, 1822
Got up this morning at four o'clock and set out with the mail coach, half past five, for Aberdeen. The fare is 5/- and 1/- to the guard and two drivers [of the] coach makes the whole 7/-. Arrived at Aberdeen half past nine. Finds the market for my commodities in a rather awkward condition. Butter being down from 64/- to 60/- and eggs also from 7 pence to 6 pence. Had some honey and wax which was an equal ill sell. Made a shift to get them bartered, the honey at 4/- and the wax 2/4, with James Dyce for drugs. Settled the greater part of my accounts—paid away about £115—and bought sundry articles that was necessary I should see personally. Carts with goods follows in the morrow.

12th February, 1822
Have been in the shop throughout the day. Sold two bolls bear for ten pints whisky, that is counting my bear at £2 and the whisky at 4/- a pint. It is Cabrach whisky from William Tocher, Mellinside.

27th February, 1822
Our Fastern's eve market this day. The weather has been good. A thin flake of snow fell early in the morning which soon dissolved without wetting the ground. The show of cattle and horses has been more limited than usual, and I believe not much business done in what there was—prices being low and also a dull sale. We have had an ordinary good market, the thinness considered. Have not drawn so much money as usual, but suppose we have our own share, and the whole passed over without fight or squabbling. The market has been custom free and also the laird affords the constables their dinner and a drink to patrol the market, keep peace, and prevent depredations.

28th February, 1822
This day have been idle—that is today have done nothing beyond shop keeping and reading the *Journal* . . . Afternoon replacing things removed in consequence of the market.

2nd March 1822
Have been making box for washing potatoes. Spent some time with
Mr Bruce and Neil.

9th March, 1822
Afternoon, Mr Neil paid me eight pounds to the credit of his lodgings
account, and in consequence had to spend some time treating him
with a few glasses punch.

29th March, 1822
Have got in about twenty-six pints whisky from Gordonstoun, price
2/7 to 2/8, the gauger being at Old Meldrum at an excise court.

2nd May, 1822
Have been considerably employed in the shop this day with the wives
from the Hillhead hose merchant. That and making preparations for
travel to Auchterless the morrow has made up the greater part of my
day's work.

4th May, 1822
Have not got much done to account this day. Our folks having a
dinner to prepare for a burial passing from Crichie of Deer to Rayne.
A man of the name of Mennie, late in Mains of Blackford. Had to
assist with raiding up the room for, and taking in, horses . . . Masons
continue building stable.

7th June, 1822
Got in about two and a half ankers Cabrach whisky this morning at
two o'clock from Charles Meldrum at £3.10 the anker.

9th June, 1822
As soon as up and in dress went into company with a marriage
party here. A James Welsh, a stone dyker (from about Deeside,
who has been at Fyvie for the last three years), to Margaret Strachan,
daughter of the late James Strachan, Cardenwell. The man's party
is collected here, and when united both parties dined here, about
sixteen in number.

19th June, 1822

Am nearly steadily employed this day packing eggs. They are a bad trade at present. Buying at 3 pence with a half penny commission to the wives and carrying them to Aberdeen and selling them at the same money with a small allowance of about penny more, which is all my pay.

28th June, 1822

Out at Auchterless this day collecting butter, price 7 pence the twenty-eight ounce pound, that is exactly a farthing the ounce. Bought about sixteen or eighteen stone's eggs, 2½ pence the dozen. Had some thunder this afternoon and about an hour's heavy rain, in the time of which while loading my cart at Redhill, broke one of the shafts by which means I was under necessity of unloading and leaving my goods, but by erecting a temporary shaft brought home the cart and sent for the goods next morning.

1st July, 1822

The boy has been cleaning out the barn to make room for laying down steeped bear to be malted . . . Have steeped five bolls bear. Sends one and a half bolls to my father to be made privately, makes the rest myself.

28th September, 1822

Carts home from Aberdeen about half past six . . . Sent three skeps of comb honey at this time which cost me 2/9 a pint and is sold at 3/-, although I was calculating on 4/- or 4/3, the price I sold at last fortnight. There was also a few pounds more taken off . . . I am left with about my own money without any expenses. The article it appears is to be an ill concern.

30th September, 1822

Have orders to prepare a dinner on Wednesday for a party of gentlemen that is to be here with a burial.

1st October, 1822

Arranging boxes, casks, etc. in the long shade and lousing and laying by goods has been my work in the intervals of shopkeeping. Have also put up hooks for harness in the new stable and rings for tying the horses to, that we may be in readiness for taking in horses the morrow. Applied to Mr Watson, butler at Fyvie, for a hare which he was good enough to send me—and two brace partridges.

2nd October, 1822
This morning repaired the bell pull of the big room, also set the tables and made other preparations for receiving the burial company of a Marjory Baxter, some distant relation of the Leslies of Rothie. They came past about two and were back to dinner about three, with which our folks were a little behind. The gentlemen part of the company consisted of Badenscoth and two of his brothers, Jonathan and Robert; Mr Leslie of Warthill; Mr Jameson, Cushnie; a Captain Baxter from Aberdeen; and Mr Keith, Netherthird; with nine other country people and servants, who dined in a separate room. The bill for the whole was four pounds.

4th October, 1822
Out at Auchterless collecting butter, this day price 11 pence the pound. Eggs are 4 pence to 4½ pence . . . Man came with a horse and met me at Redhill, and in coming home he, driving the cart with the horse he had brought, turned her over on the corner of a dyke as we came down on Gordonstoun, whereby the horse was cast and the load thrown out—but no serious accident occurred, it being moonlight and a person in company assisted in setting to rights.

14th November, 1822
Put off some time this morning putting past an anker whisky, Neil not being come home from an excise court he went to yesterday.

19th November, 1822
Mr Neil, the gauger, who has been our lodger for the last sixteen months, has removed from this to Woodhead today.

14th December, 1822
Have been employed the daylight of this day running off the whisky of my backshop cask, which was not pleasing folks in consequence

of some ill tasted whisky that had been put amongst it. I replaced with two ankers from my outhouse cask and put the bad into it that it may have time to rectify itself.

30th December, 1822

Have also bought this evening an anker Highland whisky at £4, being 10/- up since a two weeks. Is said to be in consequence of ranger officers of excise being closer stationed in different districts of the country.

2nd January, 1823

Cart away by about nine o'clock. Thus is finished my last round of business for the outgone year. I consider my mind at rest for sometime when I get my fortnight or three weeks business as it were brought to a close when the collected goods are packed off, and a supply of goods for retail are ordered, which in some measure is the beginning of another round making a kind of steady revolution in the exchange of commodities.

25th January, 1823

My writing is only to say that I am idle, for except it be my shop keeping, which is not very tedious, I am doing little besides . . . My own cart not being at Aberdeen this week I am out of salt and some other little things. The salt having come duty-free the beginning of this month, the demand is such that the stock in Aberdeen is exhausted.

28th January, 1823

The duty came off salt the fifth of the present month. The thing being known long before, people had let themselves run out, which has made the demand for the new so great that it cannot be got in sufficient quantity to meet it. The price of salt before the duty came off was £2.2/- the boll of two and a half hundredweight. The same weight now is 13/6.

30th January, 1823

Cart arrives from Aberdeen in the course of the evening . . . It appears there is no salt in Aberdeen yet. My man hath brought home three pecks that he hath with difficulty gleaned amongst the street shops.

2nd April, 1823

Mr Bruce, the supervisor, and Mr Neil came here about midday. My attention mostly engrossed with them afterwards and continued in their company until night. Have had more drink than was good for me.

6th May, 1823

Out at Forgue, collecting butter . . . and eggs . . . Mr Bruce, the supervisor, being at a treat with Mr Neil, he—the supervisor— informs me that he has orders to get me summoned to a court at Huntly for hawking tea and tobacco. Also had advice eggs ½ penny down.

9th May, 1823

This morning went up to Rothie to get an affidavit signed by Mr Hay on an account due me by the late William Murray, Newmill, Auchterless, and also to have Mr Hay's advice on my prosecution for hawking. He promises to give me his interest, but from the law regarding hawking never being in force here, he cannot say how the cause will go.

20th May, 1823

The morrow being the court day at Huntly to which I am summoned for hawking tea and tobacco I wrote to Mr Allardice, Cowbairdy, soliciting his support in court, recommended myself by saying his connection, Mr Davidson in Aberdeen, was my principal merchant.

21st May, 1823

Got up pretty early this morning, made myself ready, and set out by six o'clock in company with John Troup to Huntly. Went by Cowbairdy as I had said in my letter yesterday I would call on him. He said 'we would be in a d-nt scrape altogether but would see him in Huntly', which we did after our cause was decided. We were soon called and George Troup and myself were fined a pound each and forbidden to hawk more tea and tobacco or be liable in the penalty of ten pounds, which leaves me in an awkward dilemma whether I shall leave off taking out goods or run the risk of the penalty.

17th June, 1823
Took out rather larger quantity of goods than usual and sold all. My demand for goods is considerably increased since the prosecution for hawking.

2nd August, 1823
I am in the shop the most of this day attending thereto and posting shop books, raiding and sweeping the long shade and such like . . . Have got home some printed papers published by the Aberdeenshire Agricultural Association offering premiums to those who are the best curers of butter and the most of it also. The highest premium is £21 sterling, the sixth and lowest premium is £6.6/-. I am not fully resolved whether I shall compete or not.

23rd August, 1823
This morning set to work with three folks to butter salting. Boy weighing out and myself putting in tops. Filled about fourteen firkins, there being premiums offered this season to those who in the months of August, September and October shall cure the greatest quantity of butter and of the best quality, a preference to be given to those who use small casks and best stored rock salt, both of which I have adopted [so] that, as I intend competing, there be no objections on that score to success. The premiums are given by the Aberdeenshire Agricultural Association with a view to bringing this part of the county's product to the best possible behoof.

25th August, 1823
Have been much retarded in my work by a drunken rat catcher and his wife.

29th September, 1823
Bought this afternoon, which was delivered at night, an anker and a half Cabrach whisky at about 4/4 the pint, being about 1/- of advance since I bought last June. There is some alteration takes place in the whisky laws after 10th October. Distillers are allowed after that time

to work on paying a trifling duty in respect of what has been paid for some time past, and in consequence there will be a greater number of distilleries.

4th November, 1823

Out at Forgue . . . Am home by about eleven night. Have notice I am again to be prosecuted for hawking.

15th November, 1823

Have advice this morning of the event of the butter competition, which took place yesterday at Aberdeen, from which it appears I am awarded the sixth premium of six guineas. This is the least and last of the premiums, there being six given, but notwithstanding I have a kind of triumph over higher sounding names—my contemporaries and competitors such as Lamb, Old Meldrum; Kemp, Turriff; etc. etc., who although more extensive and older established curers must in this competition rank inferior to me. Have salted butter this afternoon. Posted books at night.

17th November, 1823

Had George Troup and his son Benjy down this afternoon consulting how we should proceed with our Huntly court business. His opinion is that if any fine is awarded we should appeal to the Quarter Sessions and wishes to consult Mr Hay's opinion on the subject. I accordingly went to call on him but did not find him.

19th November, 1823

Got up early this morning and set out to Huntly by six o'clock in company with Benjy Troup. We arrived there by ten. Our cause was not called until about two o'clock, when after considerable arguments on both sides we were awarded to be fined 10/6 each and give over hawking more tea. I proposed licensing myself at a certain place which was agreed to. We spent some time and money there, left the place at ten, home two morning. Much fatigued.

20th November, 1823

This forenoon have felt lazy and a little indisposed from yesterday's fatigue etc. Had John and Benjy Troup down consulting whether we shall rest satisfied with the decision of this court, or if we shall take the case before the Quarter Sessions. But until we are further advised none of us knows whether we can appeal or not.

21st November, 1823
My work has been raiding out long shed, turning and scraping cheese.

22nd November, 1823
This week has been rather eventful. I have been prosecuted and gratified with the publication in both newspapers of the butter competition and the merits of the lots that took premiums.

19th December, 1823
This morning bought twenty-three pints Cabrach whisky at 4/3 the pint. Have been a little scarce of that article this sometime past. The distillers, being now allowed to work at reduced duties, was expected to dry up the smuggler, which it would appear they contemplated themselves, and numbers in consequence given up. The result of which is their whisky has got scarce and has advanced 1/- a pint at least.

30th December, 1823
Was off pretty early this morning, by five o'clock, to Forgue. Have had a fair day and a great throng of business. Sold about £9 worth of goods. Butter 9 pence the twenty-four ounce and 10½ pence the twenty-eight ounce. Eggs are 6½ pence, commission included. The roads are dreadful wet. Man as usual met me at Balgavnie. Had both the horses yoked to the cart and him driving, and turning a banked corner after passing Netherthird turned over both horse and cart and all goods in a terrible wet gutter and dark night about eight o'clock. Had a lantern but in the tumble of the cart it was broke and the wind then blew out the light. I went back and got two men from Mr Keith's and succeeded in about an hour's time in putting things to rights. Had damage apiece: broke of one of the cart shafts, some eggs broke and butter a little dubbed. James Singer is my man's name.

5th June, 1824
The Saturday market of Turriff being this day we have been throng of men and horses at night.

19th August, 1824

Got up pretty early to set out to Aberdeen. It being a bad morning and raining heavy did not go so early as I otherwise would have done. Took my young mare to ride on but could not get her beyond Mill of Petty. Had to turn back and take another, which took me into town by two o'clock. Took by some goods tonight and settled some accounts etc.

20th August, 1824

The Agricultural Association being again offering premiums, am putting by a cask from each lot to wait the competition in November.

5th October, 1824

Have been partly engaged this day contriving and erecting what I call a warnist, which is a bell to awaken me when I want to be early up. She is rung by simple machinery, which is a thirty inch pendulum with a spur attached to the head of it, which spur is drawn back and fore by the vibrations of the pendulum, and every time gives the spring of bell a touch which keeps her ringing. The pendulum is suspended by a crank, and a wire runs from it to the clock thirty feet distant. At the side of the dial plate there is another crank kept in check by the end of a lever. That lever points to the hour the bell is wished to be rung at, and the lever being made so that the minute hand passes over it. When the hour hand comes round, it pushes it off which lets go the suspended pendulum and the bell sets aringing. I think the plan will succeed.

6th October, 1824

Have been employed a good part of this day finishing warnist. In the evening bringing up some accounts in old jotter book.

8th November, 1824

Went up to Rothie about twelve o'clock with an affidavit to get signed. It is concerning our butter competition—must make oath what quantity is cured, how much salt is used, and that the whole has been exhibited.

19th November, 1824

The butter competition for the premiums given by the Aberdeenshire Agricultural Association has taken place this day at Aberdeen. Am advised at night that the sixth premium of eight guineas is awarded to me. Have not heard the other particulars.

4th December, 1824

Bought two ankers Highland whisky this morning off John Grant at £4 the anker. Put one of them aside and took the other into stock; and afternoon had my stock surveyed by new supervisor, which startled me a little but met with no danger. Showed him twenty-nine gallons.

3rd January, 1825

I am in health and all my faculties sound and for the most part am employed in my shop about this season more especially, with which I sometimes consider myself much confined that I could not promise myself five or ten minutes out without some person being clambering about me, or if I am actually out, which must sometimes be the case, my wife must succeed. But to console me for my strict attention, I have this year about my ordinary success . . .

However it is all justly earned. I make a point in dealing fair with my customers and I find it is my interest to do so. I use every person civilly with little ceremony. I keep the best articles the price will afford, and my method of doing business is in selling is seldom to ask more than I take and in buying country produce I endeavour to ascertain the proper prices for the time and seldom offer less than is accepted. This method saves much time and argument and I succeed I may say to my wishes.

21st January, 1825

This day have been at Old Meldrum making excise entries, which has been my work this day. The form of entry is nearly as follows:

> OLD MELDRUM, 21st January, 1825.
> I, Adam Mackie, do hereby make entry of one barn situate on the west side of my house, marked M, for the purpose of malting; steeps in a pound 2 hundred yards west of barn; dries on the public kiln at Milton of Fyvie; keeps my dry malt in a chamber

at back of my dwelling house marked AM. This is all the places I intend to use for the above purposes until I make a new entry according to law.

Adam Mackie. Attested by Alex Barnet, office keeper.

Form of House Entry:

OLD MELDRUM, 21st January, 1825.

I, Adam Mackie, in Lewes of Fyvie, do hereby make entry of my house containing five rooms, viz. nos. 1, 2, 3, 4 and 5, for the purpose of selling porter, ale, and British spirits. Also two cellars for keeping the same, marked 6 and 7, and also one shop situated at the west end of my dwelling house for retailing British spirits, tea, coffee, snuff, tobacco etc., etc. These are all the places I intend to use for the above purposes until I make a new entry according to law.

Adam Mackie. Attested by Alex Barnet, Office Keeper.

NB. Barn and house are separate entries.

27th January, 1825

Have commenced this day taking an inventory of stock and as I intend including my whole subject it is likely to be a tedious work.

1st February, 1825

Have got about through with noting my inventory the forepart this day, and have proceeded to transcribe the same which looks like to be a day or two's work.

2nd February, 1825

Continues this day transcribing inventory with which I have got near through.

22nd April, 1825

Out in Auchterless collecting butter, price 14 pence the twenty-eight ounce pound, eggs 14 pence and ½ commission. Last when out on this round appointed a new eggs gatherer, Wiliam Ogilvie, Bogfouton, which appointment has given another of my gatherers, James Garden, so much offence that he pretends giving up working to me.

27th August, 1825
Employed this forenoon, and four of my folks, salting butter. The quality of the article is now very fine. Am giving by [sic] a cask from each lot sent to Aberdeen to compete for premium.

5th September, 1825
Had Mr Dick, supervisor of excise, here today, who has taken Mr Ogilvie's books from him and dismissed him for neglect of duty. Mr Ogilvie is a lazy gauger.

3rd November, 1825
In shop in the evening counting up what butter I have cured in the competition months and writing out an affidavit to make before a justice of the peace of the same to be sent to Aberdeen before the competition.

12th November, 1825
James Alexander, Cammaloun, marriage today. The company called here. The bride delivered of a daughter at her father's house at Woodhead this morning, consequently could not join the party . . . Have advice this day of our butter competition when I have got no prize. The first prize of thirty-five sovereigns is gained by a Mr Morrison, Baker, Peterhead.

19th November, 1825
Have been served with a summons this day to attend at a court at Huntly for hawking tea and tobacco.

22nd November, 1825
This forenoon was up at Rothie with John Troup consulting Mr Hay if he could be of any use to us against our Huntly court the morrow, which it appeared he could not except he were to go there, which he was unwilling to do on account of bad weather and roads.

23rd November, 1825
Got up this morning at half past four o'clock and was ready and set out to Huntly before six. George and John Troup in company. Mr Hay, contrary to our expectations, accompanied us and we arrived there at half past ten o'clock. There being sundry contended cases,

it was after three o'clock before we was called on, when by a few words in explanation of the word hawking by Mr Hay our case was given up. Mr Hay has the whole merit of our being taken off at this time and is entitled to our gratitude and to any other service that might be in either of our powers to do him. Took some refreshment to ourselves and set out from Huntly at about five o'clock. Stopped an hour at Burnside of Drumblade, and was home safe at eleven o'clock. Roads very bad.

7th January, 1826
Bought two ankers whisky this morning from John Rainy, Dogmoss, at £4 the anker from the Cabrach, which is still better liked than the legal.

21st January, 1826
Sent man to Old Meldrum with eleven and a quarter bolls bear on two carts. The carts was brought home at even by Thomas Hay. The man, Charles Main, on one of them dead drunk. Such circumstances makes business disagreeable.

23rd January, 1826
In the intervals of my shopkeeping this day have been at work taking up the sunk spirit cask of long shade. There being plenty of legal whisky now have no use for concealments. My man went back with a cart this morning for the ankers he lost Saturday night—two whisky and one porter. There seems to be no damage done.

15th February 1826
The bypast night we have been a good deal alarmed by Mr Neil, our late excise officer. He has been on division and distillery at Monymusk, which it appears he is not fit for managing—or whatever way it is he is wrong in the mind and very ill. We had noticed that he was a little jumbled and wished to keep him out at about twelve o'clock when he came. But he made good his entry by a window, took off his clothes, travelled in the room and knocked over the furniture and broke a dressing glass, but had not gone to bed. [He] was much raised-like when I looked in on him in the morning, with his clothes off, standing on the floor and said that the b-g-rs would not allow him to go to bed. They were holding hot irons at him. He went away to Woodhead in the forenoon.

10th May, 1826
Have been throng today or rather tonight with a crowd of people
brought together by means of a lottery (made by two Italians) of
some looking glasses and jewellery trinkets.

29th August, 1826
Have been busied measuring by and marking cloth. Have got through
with a good lot of it, but have still great lot of goods to examine and
sort by, which will hurry me for some time.

20th October, 1826
Settled up some of my Aberdeen accounts. Took coach and came to
Old Meldrum. Settled my account with the distillery and attempted
to buy more whisky from them, but did not succeed. They did not
seem disposed to take my offer of 8/- the imperial gallon . . . Came
home on foot after ten o'clock.

3rd January, 1827
The butter trade has been safe, prices being low at the outset of the
season and rose gradually whereby we had a profit in consequence of
the article advancing when on hand. Owing however to the extreme
drought which prevailed through the summer the quantity was fully
one third less than the usual make. On which account I sent butter
away only once a month in place of once a fortnight, which gave
me a little more chance of profit while prices kept advancing. I have
not been so lucky with my winter butter. Prices have fallen 28/- a
hundredweight since the middle of November, in course of which
time I have lost about £3 . . .

   Yet on the whole I conceived my business to be fully as good
as my contemporary shopkeepers and to be considerably better
than the ordinary farmer. I consider the farmer to be the source
or fountainhead of business because he is the consumer, and the
great pity is that times are not improved for him, which is also
against the merchants' interests . . . I sometimes wonder that I get
so much business as I do in a country place and surrounded with
opposition—four shops within a mile of me—and though I am in
the midst of them I think I have the best trade. I endeavour to do
my business with as few words as possible. I rarely submit to any
abatement of the price asked but at the same time I strive to have
good articles and makes the price as easy as I can. I would not take

advantage of a customer although that were in my power. I find I have an interest in being strictly honest, and my customer either does his business at once or lets it alone, which system saves much time and wrangling about prices.

20th August, 1827
Got myself ready this morning for going to Aberdeen. Went away about eight o'clock, Took man and horses with me to ·Thomas Black's. Went down on foot to Old Meldrum. Settled my porter account and bought a hundred gallons whisky at the Glengarioch Distillery at 8/- the gallon. Went on the coach to Aberdeen.

7th November, 1827
Employed in shop cutting snuff papers and making some little books.

5th January, 1828
Have again been particularly throng in shop, and a deal of business done. Carts home from Aberdeen about eleven before noon, which was lucky for me as I was run [out] of sundry articles.

12th February, 1828
Have been particularly busy this day with hose merchant's wives.

29th February, 1828
Employed in shop with wright altering some shelves and putting in some more.

Chapter 6

PROFITS, LOANS AND INVESTMENTS

3rd January, 1820
As to business, I have in some instances succeeded beyond my own expectations. I scarcely would have believed any person that would have told me ten years ago that at this time I would have been tenant in Lewes and should have rebuilt nearly all that premises in a better state than they hitherto had been, but this is the case and I have succeeded to a wonder. However this summer's trade has done me as much ill as ever my best season did me good. I think by butter alone I will lose a hundred pounds this year, which now I cannot help but by taking care in the future and making my speculations on a more limited scale.

2nd September, 1820
Delivered to my father his receipt from the bank for £100, which sum I had from him the last twelve months.

3rd January, 1821
My circumstances are in a condition that makes my life easy and comfortable and I think I enjoy as much happiness as the nature of our present state does permit.

6th October, 1821
Have at this time got out a bank receipt to George Carl for £60 I have had from him this last five or six years. Also got one for £60 to William Mackie a month since borrowed cash also.

13th December, 1821
Was in company at night with my father and George Carl. Paid him, G.C., the interest of sixty pounds I have had from him, and also given him a bank receipt for the amount.

16th January, 1822
In shop this day taking a sketch of my affairs, which have confined to shop business: and by the statement made out thirty-one and thirty-two pages of ledger it appears I am not worse in trade as there is a surplus of £73 after all claims are deducted and have only taken into account a few of the most general articles in the shop that I account the same as money. It is now three years since I took this sort of sketch at which time I was £123 in debt. The above surplus added to the debt makes me £196 better than in 1819, which is about £65 a year independent of the great sums I have been out for building the whole premises, furnishing houses and stocking the farm, which at a moderate estimate has not been less than £500, or about £83 a year for the six years I have been in Lewes. In 1815 of [sic] made old dwelling house; in 1816 took out about 500 ells stone dykes, removed and rebuilt same; in 1817 built and furnished new dwelling house; in 1819-20 the rest of the houses.

12th September, 1822
Having some spare cash by me have sent a £50 to the credit of my deposit account with the Aberdeen Bank.

15th August, 1823
Proceeded to taking by goods and settling some accounts to the amount of £80. Also deposited with the Aberdeen Bank fifty pounds, which added to former depositories since August 1822, amounts to £300, which sum I now have receipt for.

3rd January, 1824
My circumstances such as makes my mind easy. The bygone year have had sufficient success in trade, so much so that I have spared cash to my bank account £200 and that without pinching my trade. Neither do I gather near to bare my self or family, for we enjoy most of the necessaries of life and some luxuries. My table I think

I may safely say is better furnished than my contemporaries, and in dress also can bear competition. The success I meet with [on] my travelling days in the country excites so much the envy of the local shopkeepers that they have done all they could to get me suppressed, and succeeded in stirring up the excise to institute prosecutions against me for hawking tea and tobacco, and I have twice been summoned to Huntly within the last year and fined a pound, again in November and fined 10/6. These prosecutions, although with a design to hurt or suppress me, have had the contrary effect, and [in] the districts where anent the prosecutions were raised—Drumdolla, Aucharnie, and Balgavnie, all in the parish of Forgue—my trade has increased fully one third so that I have much difficulty in managing the business I have on my hands when I am there, which is a day in the fortnight during summer and a day in three and sometimes four weeks in winter. At the close of the last court I got the butter premium of six guineas given by the Aberdeenshire Agricultural Association, which though trifling in itself came opportunely to gratify my friends and gall my enemies.

4th February, 1824
I have been taking a list of goods and debts and making out a kind of statement of my affairs. I have not gone on particulars to know exactly the value of all my furniture etc., but from the sketch I have taken I find myself prosperous enough. I have £400 of spare cash in the bank, which besides furniture and stocking of farm is about my stock. I have about £110 borrowed cash and something better than £40 of credit in Aberdeen. And I consider my country debts and shop goods fully sufficient to cover the £150.

6th March, 1824
Have got a letter from Aberdeen craving arrears of Lewes, which I thought was paid. Searched the most of the forenoon for receipt, but has not got it. I now begin to think I had neglected paying.

20th August, 1824
Got on amongst my merchants [in Aberdeen] as usual until breakfast time. Then went to bank to settle my accounts. There took up £50 from Aberdeen Bank, to which I added other £50 and deposited in the Bank of Scotland, the Aberdeen Bank giving only 2½ per cent.

Have at this time £400 in the Aberdeen Bank and £100 in the Bank of Scotland.

13th December, 1824

Have advice this day from Mr Davidson, Aberdeen, that £500 he had undertaken to lodge for me in the Township cannot be taken. They had advertised they were taking interest down from 5 to 4 per cent and all those not choosing to take the latter were desired to come and receive their money, from which it was supposed there would be some that would withdraw their money. But from the present low rate of interest given by the banks—2½ per cent—few had thought of taking up. Consequently there was no room for mine although the people thought there would.

18th December, 1824

Mr Davidson writes me by my cart that he can get no place for the cash he had proposed getting into the Township, and returns two of my bank receipts. But have a letter from about same time by post saying he had found a good place with capital security, viz. Provost Brown and Son. He recommends them much. I have considered the subject on both sides and with a little reluctance have allowed him to give it them—£500 sterling at 4 per cent.

3rd January, 1825

I have had this year about my ordinary success, and notwithstanding some heavy expenses have been able to put £200 to my deposit account, the amount of which at present is £600, £500 of which took up from the bank at 20th December last and gave to Provost Alexander Brown and Son, Aberdeen, at 4 per cent the banks taking the interest to 2 per cent. I had a little reluctance in trusting my money with these people, but did it by the advice of Mr William Davidson, Aberdeen, I having employed him to put it into the Township or Shoremaster and his applications to those places (who could not take it) let Provost Brown know he had the disposal of such a thing, which he wanted for a son that was getting a share of some large manufactory about Aberdeen. Mr Davidson writes it is the best personal security to be got, the old man having an income of £2,000 for being a distributor of stamps.

My savings sufficiently explain that I have a good country trade. It is even a wonder that I can save so much after taking off the expense of my house and family which is considerable.

25th January, 1825
Have wrote this day to Mr Davidson, Aberdeen, for his advice concerning a new bank that is advertised, if he thinks it advisable that I should take a share and get their terms explained.

27th January, 1825
Have advice from Mr Davidson concerning my bank share, which is that the company are now asking £5 premium on each share, except [unless] at a meeting of leading members the applicant is thought to be a useful partner. In consequence my application must wait the trial of another meeting. The shares are £500 each.

31st March, 1825
Have been in Aberdeen all this day and employed taking by [sic] goods. Have also added £50 to my deposit account with the Bank of Scotland.

4th April, 1825
Went away at one o'clock to Old Meldrum to a meeting of distillery partners there to sign the contract and pay up the first instalment of the share I hold. The concern is divided into forty shares of £50 each, this first instalment is £20 a share. The distillery is situated on the north east side of Old Meldrum close by the manse: to be called the Glengarioch Distillery and the business to be conducted under the firm of Ingram, Lamb & Co. I left the meeting a little before ten o'clock and was home about twelve.

28th May, 1825
I sent at this time £40 as part of my first instalment of bank share, bidding Mr Davidson put too other £10 which makes £50, the amount of the first payment to be required the 6th June.

13th June, 1825
The forenoon this day have been detained a two or three hours at Fyvie paying rent, £45.1/-, which settles for last year's crop. Have also this day paid another instalment on distillery share, £15, and this day week the 6th inst. paid first instalment of bank share, £50, being in whole £110 in seven days—a considerable sum from such a small business as mine without taking up any cash from deposit. Rest of day employed making out accounts.

3rd January, 1826
As to business, I have this year had fully my usual success, having added to my deposit £225 sterling. I doubt whether many of my contemporaries can tell the same story. Of this money £100 is deposit in the bank, £75 laid out in payment of a bank share, and £50 in payment of a distillery share—that is the Glengarioch of Old Meldrum.

6th March 1826
This day have been at Old Meldrum at a general meeting of the partners of the Glengarioch Distillery, when a new committee has been elected for conducting the business and some new regulations adopted as to better management of the work, the different opinions on which subjects occupied several hours in discussing. The meeting did not finally break up until twelve o'clock. Spent an hour or two in company with my neighbour, Mr Singer in Morgan's, and then Singer and me came home in company. I was at my house safe and sound at four morning.

23rd September, 1826
Laid into the Town and County Bank £100 per Mr Davidson.

3rd January, 1827
As to business my success has been much the same as usual. I have put two hundred and some odd pounds to my deposit account, which is a profit that may be considered sufficient for a country retail trade.

24th January, 1827
I have made a finish of my statement of affairs, which turns out to be satisfactory enough. I make my whole property at this time worth £1,700, which is fully £400 more than my last inventory this time two years.

5th March, 1827
Was out this day at Old Meldrum at the general meeting of the partners of the Glengarioch Distillery, which took place as usual at Mr Barnet's. The principal business before the meeting was an advance of £10 per share to be made by the partners as the present funds seems inadequate to carrying on the business. The

same was agreed to with one dissenting voice—William Lamb—
who it was understood would submit also. By the balance sheet
of the company's affairs there appeared to be £559 in favour of
the company. There were about twenty of the partners present. I
spent the evening with them until after one o'clock. Was home
about three.

3rd January, 1828

Our trade has done about as well as usual and we are provided for
to our utmost wish. My business on the whole succeeds wonderfully,
more especially considering the growing opposition in all quarters
both at home and when I travel out. My present deposits and joint
stock shares amounts to upwards of £1,340, besides I may say a
deposit of twenty casks of summer butter in Aberdeen unsold,
which should make the above sum £1,400. I doubt much whether
my neighbour shopkeepers have similar success.

16th January, 1828

In shop making out a statement of my affairs, which is so far
satisfactory that I find the value of my property increased about
£300 since this time last year.

Chapter 7

FARMER, GARDENER AND BEEKEEPER

10th July, 1819
Boy at Aberdeen. Myself cleaned out the common stable and cow byre. Afternoon raked and put up in tramped cocks the two year old hay. Finds it not above a third crop in consequence of the great frosts and drought in the fore part of summer.

7th August 1819
There is an appearance of an excellent crop on the ground. The bear spotting occasioned by the drought is expected to mend up now considerably with the rain.

14th August, 1819
Sold a two year old stot to Alex Cowie at eight guineas . . . Cast peats, brought home twelve loads. Men cleaning out new barn and making floor. Thacking at this time finished by Charles Craig and his man:

> The new barn with broom—3 roods 4 yards at 6/-
> Dwelling house with broom and straw from the west-end to kitchen lum backside—1 rood 9 yards.
> Shop south side with broom—28 yards
>   Total 5 roods 4 yards at 6/-   £1.10.8
> Backside of the shop and chamber done with
>   straw—2 roods 7 yards. at 4/-   £0.8.6
>   £1.19.2

This is what the work costs besides affording the men their meat and labourers attending them.

23rd August, 1819

Have begun shearing bear again this day. Finds that it is too long of shearing, being dead in the straw. Corn is also ready and we must endeavour to persevere. It hath mostly all riped together. My bear is not thought so good as it should be owing to the great drought. It hath been a little hastened in the riping. The straw is rather too soft. The weather is calm and the heat intense. A burning sun.

3rd September, 1819

This day is Bartle Fair: is an excellent dry day. I have taken in 4 rucks corn and not gone to the market, my new man and two horses being at Aberdeen. I have been assisted by my father and George Carl. I have also this day sold a two year old quey at £7. I think she will be about seventeen or eighteen stone. Cattle is at present considered to be very dear.

11th September, 1819

Men thatching rucks this day and yesterday and are now all finished—the haughs being excepted—and have in ten good corn rucks and four bear. The harvest generally speaking is nearly finished and taking it on the whole what is past I have never seen a better.

17th September, 1819

This day I have finished the shearing of my corn, having had about ten people employed. It is the corn on the black ground on the Saughbog etc. and it is by all appearance a very fine crop.

3rd April, 1820

Have taken off skep eeks and cut the combs found there. Honey to the board. First day I have seen [the] bees work.

23rd April, 1820

Bees working very fine this two or three warm days.

7th June, 1820

Had a task this forenoon taking a wild kind of quey to Kirkton's bull. Shut it up with him for the forenoon, took it home and got it and another blooded afternoon. Turnip land is harrowing. James Craig threshing bear.

8th June, 1820
Took brown cow to Pettie's bull.

15th June, 1820
Afternoon, went to Fyvie Castle with rent, £35. 1/-, which with £40 paid at Martinmas settles for the bygone year of 1819. These are the first rents that have been collected at the castle in my time. Plenty of meat and drink afforded six others and myself. Had a private invitation and spent the afternoon over a mug of punch.

16th June, 1820
One bee hive cast out many drones.

27th July, 1820
A second swarm bees off this morning. Did not expect them. Had stock hives all eeked to settle them up for a season.

31st July, 1820
Old bear begun to be threshed out this day by a George Sinclair at one shilling the boll, meat, drink and lodgings afforded.

15th August, 1820
Black horse ill with a swelling in one of his hind legs. Man took him to dykeside and got him blooded.

26th August, 1820
Sold one swarm bees this day to Jonathan Forbes, dyker, my latest one (10th July), price settled 27/- which with 1/- added from me pays him for building Pumfold dykes, which is his charge.

8th September, 1820
Weather very fine. Harvest begun in general. My folks have finished all the ripe corn today having had two scythes with five people keeping tight behind for four days. Have nothing more to do now

but Saughbog, part of Claybutts and Midhow. The crop seems to be excellent.

15th September, 1820
I went to the Wood of Rothie with my father and boy and took out nearly forty trees. Brought home two cart loads . . . Observed one hive bees robbing another. After ascertaining the robbers by means of whitening cast on them, I killed the robbers and the robbed. They seem to be middling for honey. Have drained one but not yet weighed.

19th September, 1820
Killed an old hive and drained the honey. 18 pounds English. She did not swarm neither [*sic*] this summer.

29th September, 1820
Weather has a settled appearance again. Went out, set up stooks which are tolerable condition. Begun leading at twelve o'clock. Have taken in two and a half rucks from off Midhow and Saughbog, which finishes this year's crop and is a good one. The last also is in as good order as the first. Have four middling size rucks off the Howes, say from foot Londie's Brae to Ythan. There is sixteen rucks in all bear and corn supposed to average seven bolls each, i.e. 112 bolls.

20th February, 1821
Have had Johnston Skene and man this day closing in about the kiln and flooring dry corn box. Snow is all gone today. Man at plough and the other driving up stones from Marydykes Old Houses.

21st February, 1821
Have again been engaged with Johnston and his man. Their work in kiln done. Gave them by wood to make gates to dungyard . . . Man at plough.

23rd February, 1821
Weather continues remarkably fine. Observed bees at work today— the earliest I ever remember of seeing. The hive that is at work is her that was blown over about a month ago and considerably injured. Man ploughing to my father today.

25th May, 1821
A dreadful bad day. Snow and hail nearly steady. Accompanied with terrible cold north wind. Outside work is got done only with difficulty. Corn and grass more particularly is much injured with the cold and frosts at night.

25th June, 1821
Have been assisting sacking dried corn this morning. Sent the same to Milton who refuses to do it until the middle of the week in consequence, as he says, of being two hours later than the appointment of bringing it in. Took out the corn and sent it to Mill of Petty who set to work immediately . . . My own man and John Ogilvie threshing bear.

7th July, 1821
Three carts driving peats. Thirty-four cart loads home today.

16th July, 1821
Am at work drying malt today, and working in garden between hands. Three carts driving peats: are all home today—Sixty-six loads.

18th July, 1821
A fine warm sunny day. Have had two hives swarmed today— one at nine and the other at eleven o'clock. The first after being two or three hours settled left the skep unobserved and went and lodged in the slates of the church. Went and looked at them but found it unpracticable to take them out. Two carts driving sods today.

19th July, 1821
Have been busied this day enclosing a piece of dungyard for cattle to lie in . . . The last of my sods home today, which finishes our fuel driving for the season.

24th September, 1821
A fine clear day. Have been engaged a little examining the state of bee hives, which I find is poor. Have taken the greater part of bees out of two and killed the remainder.

1st October, 1821
About eleven o'clock brought home a quey from Head Town, Netherthird, that I had bought from him at £3.15/- for a mart.

27th December, 1821
Men are taking corn to barn and hay to loft. William Cheyne here from Inverurie killing an ox of about thirty-four stone to be sold on Saturday.

29th December, 1821
William Cheyne here selling his beef which he accomplished at 4 and 5 pence the pound. Bought from me at £4.15 a quey that I have been feeding which he has also killed this evening and purposes selling on Monday.

6th February, 1822
One horse, the black, ill of a severe cold. Sent for John Steel, farrier, who prescribed some drink with antimony, sulphur, cream of tartar etc.

8th February, 1822
Man with brown horse carting away some dung. The other horse continues very ill.

13th February, 1822
Man continues driving clay with one horse, the other being still unwell.

16th February, 1822
The black horse yoked this afternoon for the first time this fortnight. He again getting better.

11th March, 1822
This day have been employed a good deal assisting at training two stots to work in the harrow. They are three year olds and have not been in halters before. One of them has been very wild but we have succeeded in breaking them a little.

13th March, 1822
Went out for an hour or two in the forenoon and assisted with yoking of stots who are likely to come too to work with little more trouble. Man at plough.

15th March, 1822
Assisted the boy with the stots, who are getting quite tractable.

21st June, 1822
Bees looking like swarming and one has cast a first, the other a second, swarm. Put off a good deal of time going between shop and garden. Alex Milne with about six or eight men begun straightening the water from the bridge to the upper end of my land, to which the new cut was brought two or three years ago. It looks to be no advantage to me. In the first place they dig down and cover my water bank grass, which is a considerable loss in this season of drought. In the next place they take an acre and a half of my Saughbog off for which I am not likely to be well paid.

19th July, 1822
The afterpart of the day prepared boards and eeks and eeked seven bee skeps, which took some time to adjust them right, and the bees pursuing me in swarms. The weather appears to be agreeable for them. They are thriving well. The boy and John Walker . . . are hoeing turnips, which crop is looking well since they got the rain.

27th August, 1822
My horse grew unwell coming down on Netherthird which I feared, and turned out to be, gravel. He came on to near Shait Brae when in spite of all my efforts he lay down in the cart. I got him loused with some difficulty and led him home. George Florence, Gordonstoun, went with a horse for my cart and brought her home. My horse continued all the way. I had difficulty keeping him and [he] lay down once and tumbled for some time.

28th August, 1822
Sent man away this morning for Juda's eggs, and the rest to the scything and they got finished by taking cliack a little after one o'clock. It is all cut now but no corn nor bear into the yard. The crop will not be bulky.

12th September, 1822
Have also smoked four bee hives and finds them but poorly supplied with honey. Middling hives averaging I think three and a half pints honey each.

24th September, 1822
Man is at Tarves with my Bartle Fair colt, it having got an ill character for being wrong in the legs, for which reason I did not think it proper to keep him. He is sold at £12. I lose about £2 or £2.10/-.

16th November, 1822
I intended going to the Turriff Feeing Market to engage a new man but have settled with my present one, John McDonald, at £6.10/-, being a pound less than he has had from me the last three half years by gone. Fees at the market today are said to be from £4.10 to £5 for men. All kind of farm produce are now so low that servants and other things must come down.

1st May, 1823
Was considerably interrupted with one of the stots getting himself worried on a potato. Sent for John Ironside who cleared the gullet by putting down a rope.

7th August, 1823
The weather being fine this morning, I put eeks on four bee skeps that have not swarmed. The wet and coldness of the season has been against them. Only one swarm out of six thriving hives.

27th September, 1823
This is a fine fair day again. My folks are shearing at pieces of lying corn that could not rightly be got up with scythes. They are intending getting cliack, which was accomplished by about six o'clock. Have no corn in yet.

2nd February, 1824
Sent carts away to Macduff this morning with twenty bolls meal sold at 15/- the boll. Grain is now looking up—could now get 16/-.

20th February, 1824
Have been interrupted a little with a stot that has been swelled two or three times on the turnip. Put some oil and gin over his throat.

30th June, 1824
Have been out at Turriff Market looking for a young horse and have met in with one—a black mare, three years old at £24 from Mr Jameson, Cushny, Auchterless. I intend her to relieve my brown horse who is sometimes liable to a gravel. He is now nine years old, being three when bought in Bartle Fair in 1818. My black horse is now about seven years old, being three years bought in Cowan Fair, Turriff, 1820. Have this day also sold three stots at £12 and bought less and leaner at £9.5/- —three of them.

3rd September, 1824
Went to Bartle Fair after breakfast to try to buy some cheese but found them dearer than I afford, being from 5/- to 5/9. Bought two queys to be winter marts, and settled my porter account with Alex Morrison, Old Meldrum. It has been a fine day, a large market and the greater part of the cattle sold. I made a small mistake which occasioned me a little inconvenience. Forgot to take any money to market with me. Was supplied by Alex Cowie from Head Town, Auchterless.

28th February, 1825
Went out afternoon assisting at the training of a stot. Made very little progress with him. Could not get him to keep on his feet.

5th August, 1825
Was up calling on George Carl senior, who has got himself hurt by a drive of a bull at Kirkton.

28th October, 1825
In the forenoon was over at John Steel's, Cromblet, with the young mare, she having taken some trouble in her mouth and throat that we did not rightly understand. He called it a sore throat and took some blood from one of her hinder thighs.

21st June, 1826
Employed putting some posts into the paling at the corner of garden next the bridge. Have also had some trouble with a swarm of bees that came off about ten o'clock, settled and went up into the skep well enough, but came out again about one, and all our efforts to make them light again proved useless. They went in the direction of Fyvie Castle. Followed them to the wood on this side the lake where they crossed. I gave them up then and returned home. In the afternoon heard of some swarms lighting about the castle, but as I once lost sight of them shall not mind them more.

4th July, 1826
Have trifled away the principal part of this day to little account. Was interrupted for some time taking a swarm bees out of the top of a tree.

5th August, 1826
Have three of my folks at Fyvie paying bondage. From the Aberdeen Chronicle observes the harvest begun south, and north is said to be the earliest in the memory of man.

2nd October, 1826
Have taken up our potatoes today. They are a fair crop.

4th November 1826
Have been occupied part of my time this day planting out some flower roots in garden.

7th March, 1827
Was also out assisting at dressing some seed corn.

14th May, 1827
I have been working and scraping a good deal in garden today . . . Man ploughing my in turnip land.

29th May, 1827
My servants are all leaving me this term and the new ones only comes home tonight the first of them.

27th June, 1827
Man cropping corn that looks like over-growing itself in this fine weather. J.O. gravelling garden paths anew. Boy pulling docks, thistles, etc.

5th September 1827
Assisting with cattle, my folks being still employed at corn cutting.

12th September, 1827
The weather has been so very fine for the last two or three days that corn seems in excellent order for leading, and we have accordingly taken in all this day from breakfast time.

18th September, 1827
My folks are at cutting the corn of Saughbog, which they have finished, and is cliack for this season.

7th November, 1827
My folks planting turnips.

2nd February, 1828
Pruning berry bushes as also planting cuttings of bushes.

PART III

Country Life

4. Where Adam farmed. Lewes Farm, Fyvie

Chapter 8

LOCAL AFFAIRS

12th May, 1818

The Methlick Water, now so far famed, is discovered this Spring of 1818, or rather the qualities of the water discovered. The wonderful virtues of this water (or that is attributed to it) brings from all quarters great numbers of people to try if its qualities be real. It is said to be a grand antidote for the scurvy, which disease with a few washings is wholly removed. People oppressed with the stone or stony gravel find after a few applications of this water the stone dissolved. Scarcely any complaint can occur but this water is said to remove. What the virtues or qualifications of the water may be cannot easily be determined, but one thing we know for certain that great throngs of people hath attended it during the months of March and April and still continue, although not in such numbers (12 May). I am told (for I have not seen it) that there will be fifty people at it at one time. Others agree that there is not less than from fifty to sixty a day. We see cartloads of it driving in every direction to Huntly, Banff, Keith, Turriff etc., etc. All must have a trial of this all-healing water. I am told that some days there will be from fifteen to twenty carts loaded. It is sold in and about Aberdeen at 3 pence the pint, at some other places at 2 pence, and it is bought up with great avidity when the people are fully convinced that it is the real Methlick water, as some wags hath been detected filling their casks at the nearest river or burn and selling it for Methlick Water. Some Aberdeen carters hath been found in this fraud and fined accordingly. These wells are situated in the parish of Methlick on the farm of Newton occupied by George Sim—Lord Aberdeen, proprietor.

June 1819
This month a monument of marble is erected on the wall of the church in memory of General the Honourable William Gordon of Fyvie. The monument is said to cost £500—is done by a William Marshal, Edinburgh, and two men from that put it up.

15th November, 1819
Evening in shop. Put upon the middle of the night with people endeavouring to settle Van and Ingram.

16th November, 1819
Mostly in the house this day not employed to any good account. Much disturbed with Mr Jaffray settling with Van. Van claims Ingram's daughter, who is to be married to another man on Saturday, but it would appear she had wrote some love letters to Van for some time previous, which he thinks give him a right to the woman, or in other words he will stop the marriage or recover damages for breach of promise.

24th December, 1819
This day I have been up through Walls and Auchterless selling goods and collecting butter and eggs, but scarcely any getting. This day have had many enquiries about John Troup, who travels on the same road nearly. He has been bad for the last two or three weeks, being at a market at Old Rayne, 7th this month, when Adam Hay, another butter buyer from Meikle Rothie, was also, and it appears they had met or fallen into company in a house there at night, when it appears they had made some outcast and fixed in one another so that A.H. had cast J.T. into the fire and kept him in until he was so much burnt that he has not got up since.

16th April, 1820
James Gammie, my man, away seeing a woman that has brought him a daughter.

24th April, 1820
Had George Fyfe, messenger, here summoning me to circuit court.

1st May, 1820
Going to Aberdeen to meet the circuit court.

2nd May, 1820
Went down to court but no admittance but to witness's apartments. Went on my own business in the town . . . Called again at court, had admittance, and heard part of a woman's trial for child murder.

3rd May, 1820
Went up to court and heard part of the trial [of] a James Anderson for forgery: not proven. The people on whose case myself and others were, having confessed their crime and sentenced to seven years banishment, we got out leave about eight o'clock at night. I was paid 30/-. Immediately proceeded home.

15th May, 1820
Paid to the Militia Club 7/6.

29th October, 1820
James Gammie, my man, and Mary Anderson (who left service here at Whitsunday) and who is by child with him was before the session today.

9th December, 1820
Weather is moderate with a thin covering of snow. James Gammie met me with another horse at Redhill. Left him (J.G.) then in consequence of his lass, Mary Anderson, being in child labour.

26th May, 1821
This Whitsunday term both men and myself there at Turriff market. Am allowing my present man to go away for some irregular conducts between him and Mary Morrison, the kitchen maid. Have not got myself appointed a man to my mind and wish one I am acquainted with or that can be well recommended.

28th May, 1821
James Gammie and Mary Morrison both leaves there service here this day. The one has been four years here, the other two.

3rd March, 1821

Was at Mr Neil's this evening. Gardener and Grant in house when I came home. They had made some noise about Dr Argo's house and scared his women, who had alone been [*sic*]. There is like to be some litigation in consequence.

31st October, 1821

Man away settling about a child he has had at Rods.

24th March, 1822

Got myself ready this morning and went out to Gordonstoun to Elspet Allardice's burial. She was a young woman aged about twenty and has lingered in a consumption the last six months since October last. She is buried at Auchterless.

26th May, 1822

Have been at church today . . . The minister gave a discourse about singing in consequence of the precentors and some others wishing a singing master of which he did not approve. Tells us that none other shall be appointed to sing but Mr Sievewright, who hath taught here already with approbation—Sievewright [was] in the lateron at the time—and that Sievewright would attend in the church at five o'clock and converse with those on the subject who wished to be instructed. He, the minister, also took occasion to hint that ministers are under no orders to marry, baptise, or catechise out of the church, but which rule he had never availed himself of, but for the accommodation of his people had travelled thousands of miles: in return for which he had the favour to ask that there should be no parties or divisions in the singing, but that those that preferred other teachers should sing at home or in their own meetings.

I went to the church at five o'clock, when Mr Sievewright was there and about thirty or forty people, eight or nine of which put down their names as scholars; and thus ends the present stage of the business.

10th August, 1822

A young lad, shepherd to the laird of Rothie, has this day taken his own life by hanging himself. The only cause that is assigned for this dreadful act is his parents having checked him in getting some suit of new clothes, which it seems they thought could not be rightly afforded. He is said to be about seventeen years of age. His name is William Crane, son of William Crane in Springs Leys.

29th August, 1822
Got my orders ready and sent carts away to Aberdeen about eleven o'clock. A cart from Fyvie that was to go in company came past about an hour after, the man with her, George Masson, got himself hurt by letting his horse turn and not having hold of him when he was affrighted at meeting some people on the road - an evil in consequence of not having a rope at the horse head.

24th October, 1822
The forepart of this day I have been busily employed making out my Aberdeen orders to let me away to John Cowieson, Rods, marriage. I got through with my work by one o'clock and in dress by two when we went (that is Mr Neil, Ferguson, Bruce, my wife and self) and joined them at church. Went home with them and stopped until ten o'clock when a cart of my own whom I had appointed came and took us all home. The night was something wet. Rods had a very good dinner but was too long in bringing any toddy—say six o'clock—when some were beginning to murmur.

30th November, 1822
A person of the name of William Littlejohn, a son of the late Andrew Littlejohn, Mains of Crichie, has been buried at the churchyard this evening, who is said to have hung himself. The cause assigned is said to be by being embarrassed with natural children. He had been married and lived near Mill of Tochel, and was a widower at the time of his death.

6th January, 1823
My folks who have leave from work on this Christmas Day and employs their time in getting drunk.

10th January, 1823
Had an invitation to drink tea and spend the evening at James Carl's. My wife went at six and I followed at eight. Got some coarse whisky punch and haddocks.

1st February, 1823

Shopkeeping and other trivial affairs hath occupied my attention the forepart of this day. At one o'clock went out to George Ironside's marriage, who is married to Jane Milne, daughter of William Milne, Mill of Pettie. There was a large company—perhaps not under six score—when both parties were united. There was a considerable fall of wet kind of snow the forepart of the day. Was succeeded with frost in the afternoon and evening. In consequence of the wetness of the day I set my folks to the flail, but I believe they rather employed themselves shooting at the marriage.

20th February, 1823

My wife has been out all the bypast night at her sister's accouchement—my brother's wife. It appears she was delivered this morning of [a] dead female child. The mother is in an ordinary way . . . My wife was again taken away this forenoon to James Munro's wife, who it seems is also taken in labour.

21st February, 1823

James Munro is absent on account of his wife's labour, which it would appear is tedious. We hear Dr Torry has been with her twenty-four or thirty hours, and this evening has artificially delivered her of a dead child, which is said to have been so for two weeks, mortification being begun.

22nd February, 1823

J. Munro's wife we are told was relieved from her sufferings by death this morning. Her case is an afflicting one, the poor creature had suffered terribly and destitute of many of the comforts necessary for her situation.

> How swiftly life doth pass
> How soon the night comes on
> A train of hopes and fears
> And human life is gone.
>
> Then may we daily seek
> A mansion in the skies
> Where summers never cease
> And Glory never dies.

17th April, 1823

Have been at work this morning and forenoon making up goods for taking out the morrow. About twelve o'clock went out to Miss Milne's marriage, Geldingsburn, who is married this day to James Duguid, wright. The company consisted of about 60 or 70 folks. I assisted at serving up the dinner at the people's request. Came home between six and seven and finished my preparation for travel the morrow.

14th May, 1823

A woman named Anne Craib is left here by an Aberdeen chaise, who as soon as it was gone told us she was come to be a dependant on the parish.

27th June, 1823

The laird of Rothie, James Leslie, is buried at Fyvie this day in great pomp. He is brought down in an Aberdeen hearse drawn by four horses. Fourteen chaises followed, his tenants on foot brought up the rear. There being no part of their family buried here before, he caused a tomb be erected at the front of the church towards the east end. It was begun to [sic.] about the latter end of May and finished much about the time of his death.

4th July, 1823

Spent a good part of my time with Dr Argo's, who are removing from their house here on Maryfield. Their house and all its fixtures are taken off their hand by the laird at a valuation, which came to about £120. Their crop is also taken at a valuation so they have no errand back here.

Indolence (in my opinion) has been the overthrow of Dr Argo in Fyvie. Himself, his brother and some others, after their house was locked up, came down and took some dinner here. They after went the length of Woodhead with Mr Neil, gauger, where they intended to lodge for the night.

7th February, 1824

Have account of a fire at Cottown, Fetterletter, that happened yesterday afternoon when the dwelling house of William Coburn, shoemaker there, was entirely consumed and all his furniture and corn rucks. The fire occasioned by some fire falling on the roof from the chimney of an adjoining house (his shop).

9th February, 1824
Subscribed 10/- to the folks canvassing for William Coburn, whose house was burnt.

28th March, 1824
An instance of the afflicting hand of Providence is at present in this neighbourhood. The wife of Robert Henry, merchant, Woodhead, was this day week safely delivered of a child and continued in a fair way for a two or three days, then took some sudden turn and has died this day. What adds to the melancholy case is that himself last Friday night was attacked with a rose in his thigh, which has cast him into a dangerous fever.

31st March, 1824
Robert Henry, Woodhead, whose wife died on Sunday, is himself dead this day, and their young child also died yesterday. This is the most afflicting case that ever happened in this neighbourhood in my day. Man, wife and child, three dead bodies in one house at one time. I understand they have left five children alive behind, the oldest girl about thirteen.

19th April, 1824
I have been all this day at Woodhead assisting the friends of the late Robert Henry in taking an inventory of his subject. It has been a tedious kind of work, the goods being in such confused order.

2nd May, 1824
Was at church. Text, Judges, 1 Chapter, 7 Verse: 'As I have done, so God hath requited me'. A subject tending to show that the workers of iniquity often meet with the punishment of their crime even in this life as was the case with Adonibezek and many others whom he named. The subject not being of the usual form is supposed by some to allude to a trial before the circuit court from this parish of a James Philip for wilful fire raising at Bogdavie, a ruck of hay belonging to Alexander Rainy there being burnt in October last. Rainy accused Philip of raising the fire. Philip was Rainy's subtenant—that is he had a house from him—and they had been on ill terms before the fire

commenced. Philip has been at large the most of the time on bail. His trial came last week when he was acquitted. It was the opinion of most people that Rainy had raised the fire himself and accused Philip in order to get his vengeance wreaked on him. The minister (who was at the trial) it would appear has also embraced the same opinion.

11th June, 1824

My time has been taken up this day with the Lady Mrs Gordon's burial. The whole of the Fyvie tenants of Mr Gordon were invited. We assembled at the Mains of Fyvie at twelve o'clock, got a good dinner there, and then went over to Sunnyside about three o'clock. As soon as the body was got into the hearse the procession moved from that in nearly the following order: first, two boys neatly dressed in black with long white cravats hanging down over their waists; two men in deep mourning carrying cross headed poles covered with a long piece of black cloth and black sashes over their shoulders tied below the other arm; the hearse drawn by six horses covered with black; Mr Gordon's chaise and four horses followed by other seven chaises drawn by two horses each; the whole closed with about 250 tenants on foot four abreast. She is laid in the grave above the general, her coffin about six inches above his supported by oaken trestles. The stone is then lowered by means of pulleys. She is said to be eighty years of age; Mr Gordon, her son, is said to be now 49 years. I remember her marriage to the general. It was in July, I think, about sixteen or seventeen years ago. The church bells have been rung steady, with the exception of Sunday, since the morning of the 3rd. Her husband, General Gordon, was laid in the same grave eight years ago.

11th October, 1824

A little time spent with a Mr Brown, who has been here since Saturday. He is taking some kind of a survey of the county and soliciting orders for a book called *A Scots Directory*.

7th January, 1825

As has been the case this some days past, I am in my shop and busily employed. This day ends Christmas, which my men folks had need of. They travel and drink by turns day and night. Their liberty at this time distresses them much.

24th February, 1825

We hear there had been some squabbling and fighting at George Troup's about the middle of the night, when Alex Craib, Parkburn, and John Coburn, Fetterletter, had overlaid a man of the name of Robb from Old Deer to that degree that his life is in danger.

16th April, 1825

Man complains of being unwell.

There has been a militia ballot at Turriff this day when seventeen from this parish has been drawn. The most part of the men liable have joined the parish club, subscribing 10/- apiece, thereby giving mutual protection. I have been employed by some merchants in Aberdeen calling themselves the Militia Insurance Association as an agent to distribute these protections here at 15/6, each giving protection for one year. Have insured twenty-four men and hears there is only one of them drawn, viz. a Henry Cruickshank, Woodhead, Fyvie.

1st August, 1825

A report having gone out that one of our maids, Cirsty Scattertie, is with child to our lodger, Dr Chalmers, have called both to account today on the subject. They both admit being connected, but the woman thinks she is not with child. I intend having them parted as soon as I conveniently can.

13th September, 1825

When I came home from Forgue this night had accounts of a woman calling herself Helen Campbell who had been attempting to issue forged notes on the Aberdeen Bank, but who had been detained and kept in custody by George Carl and William Urquhart, constables, the latter of which and myself sat up with her through the night, and George Carl accompanied by his son James with a cart took her away to Aberdeen by four o'clock in the morning.

11th February, 1826

I was out in the forenoon and afternoon at the funerals of Mrs Milne and Mrs Rait, the wife of Charles Rait, grieve at Fyvie Castle, and her mother. A case I have not before witnessed a similar. The mother and daughter both cut off in one night (by putrid sore throat), and what makes the case more affecting is the man's whole family cut off about the same time. A child of about eighteen months old died four weeks ago. The mother near her confinement at the time bore another child two weeks after the death of the first. This second child lived about four weeks, was buried Tuesday last. And what still adds to the survivor's affliction is the death of a natural child he had to the south of Aberdeen—a boy now about twelve years of age and buried the same day his youngest child was [buried] here. May we be taught by such afflicting dispensations of Providence to be in preparation for our final departure hence.

22nd February, 1826

Was roused from bed this morning by one of the girls coming ben, saying Bell Rose was over saying her father was found dead on the road. Got up as fast as I could and went down the turnpike road after the folks, and found what was reported to be actually true: that he was found dead in the ditch on the upper edge of the road about three hundred yards past the turn opposite Burngarnie. He had been the worse of drink, had fallen on the road and by the impressions in the dub was supposed to have struggled a good deal. His two daughters, Bell and Sally, were agitated in the extreme, especially the latter. He was carried to his own house on boards. I waited and assisted at taking off his clothes, which were all over with dub, both back and breast. This is a case that throws his daughters into deep affliction and must also perplex them how to keep a Toll Bar and Post Office. I feel much for them. I was employed the rest of the day packing eggs—had proposed sending them to Aberdeen this week—but as I thought myself throng before, my neighbour's accident nearly defeats my purpose. Have done at them what I could through the day and evening. Sat up at walking of Mr Rose's body to near five morning.

23rd February, 1826

In the forenoon had to prepare myself for two funerals: that of Mary Morgan, a girl who hath died at Fyvie Castle where she had been a servant. She was the daughter of the general's black groom by Nannie Durno, who was also serving there at the time. The other funeral is that of my neighbour Mr Rose. The company, with the exception of the women, met here and got their entertainment, there not being room at the Toll Bar House. The interment was over about five o'clock. I came home and made preparations as fast as I could for sending carts to Aberdeen and got them away about ten o'clock. Went over and slept in the Toll House.

24th February, 1826

Was over in the evening with the Misses Rose at the engaging of a boy of James Cruickshank's to keep the Toll Bar for them. Went back and slept in their house. Sally is very unwell. Was not stout before and their present misfortune has made her worse.

26th February, 1826

Have paid two visits to the Misses Rose at the Toll Bar today. Was also twice there yesterday, condoling with them under their recent affliction.

28th February, 1826

Was over at the Misses Rose in the evening. Their acquaintance, a James Moir, coach guard, then came over and took a bed here.

1st March, 1826

In the evening was also over a little at Toll Bar, writing the Post Office, Edinburgh, of Mr Rose's death.

7th March, 1826

Was also over this afternoon at the Toll Bar with William Urquhart, taking an inventory of their furniture etc.

19th April, 1826

Was over at the Toll Bar in the evening hearing a settlement between the Miss Rose's and their boy, Jock Cruickshank, who had left them. He had forfeited his wages, and [they] took the half, 10/-, which they proposed giving to the poor.

22nd April, 1826

The Toll Bar is taken today at Turriff by John Pratt, tailor, at £72. New neighbours which we fear will not be as agreeable as the old.

24th April, 1826

This morning before seven o'clock my wife, her sister Helen and Charles Main our servant man is set out to Aberdeen as witnesses in the case of Helen Campbell that was apprehended here for uttering forged notes.

26th April, 1826
Have some advice this morning from the circuit court that the wife
[that] our folks was summoned anent has pleaded guilty and received
sentence of transportation for seven years . . . My wife was paid
10/- a day— 30/-; each of the rest with 7/6- —22/6. Our lodger, Dr
Chalmers, and Dr Pirie from Turriff, who was in on a case of rape,
was each paid six guineas, and their criminal got off by means of an
error in his indictment.

3rd September, 1826
This afternoon I spent in making a visit to see Alexander Nicol,
Burreldales. He has been distressed a year or two with a cancer in
his nose, which has now grown to a size that nearly covers his face.
He is very weak now and has been confined to bed for the last twelve
months nearly.

11th September, 1826
Have been out this day from ten to two o'clock at the funeral of
Alexander Nicol, Burreldales. He has been distressed for the last two
years or so with a cancer in his nose. His body is interred at Fyvie.

15th June, 1827
There was some disturbance at home today with a vagrant boy
calling himself William Leith, who stole my wife's pocket book out
the window of sleeping closet backside the house. They followed
him to Mr Wilson's, took him back and took the money and some
other trinkets from him and dismissed him.

21st July, 1827
Was out this forenoon a three or four hours at another burial—
Margaret Cruickshank, the wife of John Troup, Merchant, Hillhead.
She has died of consumption leaving her husband and nine children,
some of them quite young.

23rd July, 1827
Have been out this day at the burial of William Crichton, Bogtama.
He was interred at Auchterless. I accompanied the procession to the
Hill of Seggat and came home by Burreldales to ask for two of their
people who are lying in typhus fever.

28th July, 1827

This day I have been out at the burial of the goodwife of Burreldales, the widow of the late Alexander Nicol. She has died of typhus fever. One of her daughters is also lying, but is expected to get over.

20th December, 1827

Had a funeral party for a short time today of Baillie James Webster from Banff. The people stopped a short time and took some wine and fed horses. James Brown, our kirk bellman, is cousin to the deceased and his nearest of kin, and if there is no will made conveying the subject away otherwise, he will of course succeed to what property there is.

14th February, 1828

The account of Mr Hay's death, which happened at Aberdeen this morning, has cast a general gloom on this neighbourhood. He was a much respected gentleman and deserved to be so. He went to Aberdeen about three weeks ago for the benefit of medical advice and there was little transpired here concerning the state of his health until Monday last that Mr Chalmers came of express for the Misses Hay, his sisters. Since that time there has been an intense anxiety in this place to hear how he was, and this day has brought the fatal news

16th February, 1828

The remains of Mr Hay is brought home today. About sixty people, me among the rest, went out the road perhaps near about a mile and met the procession and accompanied it to Rothie. The folks were chiefly from this neighbourhood, Rothie and Monkshill, and went without invitation. Mr Thain, schoolmaster, suggested this turn out as a mark of respect to the deceased.

22nd February, 1828

This day have been at the funeral of Mr Hay, Mickle Rothie. The party consisted of all the tenants of Monkshill and Fyvie Estates, perhaps about a hundred and forty, besides a company of from forty to fifty gentlemen. He was intended to be carried to the churchyard, but in consequence of the extreme wetness of the roads a hearse was procured. It was followed by ten chaises and a number of riders, the tenants mostly on foot. He was laid down about three o'clock pm., a burial service said by Bishop Skinner, Aberdeen. The common people were all dined previous to lifting, and the gentlemen went back after the interment. Four people that digged the grave and the bellman was [*sic*] dined here and got as much drink as they could take, all at the expense of the deceased.

27th February, 1828

The *Journal* notices the death of Mr Hay in the following words:

> Died here 14th inst. James Hay Esq., of Monkshill, aged 53. A Gentleman of the strictest probity and honour. A warm-hearted friend and most intelligent and extensively useful member of society. His unaffected kindness and benevolence will be long remembered in his native parish and among a very extensive circle of acquaintance.

A well wrote eulogy and which the gentleman has well deserved.

Chapter 9

A RATHER MORE INTERESTING CASE
THAN GENERALLY OCCURS AT FYVIE

17th September, 1825

I had commenced posting the day book this morning, was interrupted about ten o'clock by a man calling on our doctor with his head fractured saying that he had been nearly killed and robbed of 36/-, which was his all. He, the wounded man, calls himself Alexander McKay and [said] that he was driving cattle for David Cabel; that he was returning from Falkirk and met in with the man who struck him and robbed him on his way home at Coupar [Angus]; that they both came together to Daviot where they lodged during the last night; that the suspected man, whose name he thinks is William Allan, advised him to come along [and] that he would take him to his place nine miles distant from here and keep him, free, until Tarves market next Tuesday that his, McKay's, master came [was coming] to. They both came in company from Daviot, and at the woodside above he knocked him down with a metal headed whip. I was up at the woodside together with Mr Hay and Captain Forbes of Blackford, who happened to be here a little before the man came in. I stood by the man part of the time while his head was dressing; saw several pieces of bone taken out. The doctor says it is next to impossible that he can live as his brains are injured and part of them out. He has given some little account of the man, such as that he was newly recovered out of the smallpox; that he seemed to [be] acquainted with a man they met on the road with a cart. These are the chief things transpired yet. The man is still alive.

18th September, 1825

The present seems eventful times here. Mr John Fyfe, messenger at arms from Aberdeen, was here by two o'clock this morning, which I soon understood was in pursuit of the man suspected of the robbery. A Captain Forbes of the family of Blackford, who happened to be here at the time the wounded man came, being on a journey from Craigston to Aberdeen, and made himself a little active in inquiring after the circumstances of the robbery and apparent murder. He went and brought Mr Hay here, also took a statement of the case as far as could be gathered with him to Aberdeen; and he had put upon Mr Fyfe to go in pursuit of the person suspected. The wounded man mentioned having met a man with a cart on the road as they came from Daviot, with whom Allan seemed acquainted; and Allan mentioned to the man with the cart that he expected a summons waiting him at home to the ensuing circuit court as a witness against Adam Fordyce, to be tried at said court for issuing forged notes. This circumstance of his name being known and that he was a witness had immediately given the messenger a scent of him, which he followed out with promptitude taking William Urquhart, our messenger, along with him to Cuminestown, the place where they suspected the man lived. Had from that got notice that he was living with his wife's father some way about Griens, to which they immediately proceeded and found him keeping his father-in-law's cows, and brought him a prisoner here by 12 o'clock. This day being Sunday crowds of people have flocked about the house and up and down the road anxious for news and a sight of the prisoner.

19th September, 1825

The procurator fiscal for the county of Aberdeen, Mr Simpson, had given notice to be here this day, which he accordingly was to take a precognition of the evidence against the woman, Helen Campbell, apprehended here on Tuesday last the 13th inst. for issuing forged notes, to which case they proceeded by a little past nine o'clock. Also a precognition was taken of the case of Allan, the person in custody suspected of the robbery. Great numbers of people were called in both cases, and the fiscal, his clerk and Mr Hay continued until about nearly one o'clock the next morning steadily engaged the whole time. About same time, also one o'clock Tuesday morning, Mr Fyfe set out with his prisoner Allan locked arm and arm with Alex Alexander, constable, and himself riding behind.

The business going on about this house interrupts me in mine considerably. Weather soft and warm.

20th September, 1825

Our law gentlemen again at work today by six o'clock morning at their examinations. Was also examined myself this day—whereabout the hat was found?—which finished their business here and they left this place for Aberdeen about ten o'clock.

These transactions has kept our house a prison and a criminal court for nearly a week. We had proposals made last week for holding our harvest home on Monday night, but this business going on caused us alter our plan, but with which we proceeded this afternoon and held our ball at night. Present perhaps nearly forty folks of our neighbours. Parted about four o'clock next morning. The wounded man, who lies in one of the chamber room beds, we have gone out and into occasionally, and about midnight thought he was dying. He is weak, has been always waked through the night.

24th September, 1825

Alexander McKay, the man that came in wounded this day week, is still living but very weak—requires a person with him night and day.

26th September, 1825

Mr Simpson, procurator fiscal, here at night examining witness in the case of William Allan.

27th September, 1825

The fiscal went from here to Cuminestown making further enquiries in the case of William Allan, the suspected robber.

30th September, 1825

The wounded man, Alexander McKay, that lies with us is still living but has not spoke any since yesterday morning and moved very little. He has stood out beyond expectation.

2nd October, 1825

The man Alexander McKay who was robbed and nearly killed on Saturday 17th ult. has died this evening at about half past nine o'clock. He has been in great agony the last three days, say Thursday, Friday, Saturday, and this day. His whole faculties being gone, he has lain immovable, except when turned or altered, having alone the power of breathing, which has been driven apparently with all his force. There has been two people kept steady with him night and day.

3rd October, 1825
The dead man Alexander McKay has had his head and part of his body dissected by our own Dr Chalmers assisted by Dr Pirie from Turriff. William Milne made a coffin and we have had him interred this afternoon, about twenty of the neighbours present, Mr Hay and the minister included. I am not well aware how I shall be remunerated for the trouble and expense I have had with the man since he came here. Mr Simpson, the procurator fiscal, says it must fall on the parish, and they can have recourse to the parish the man belonged to, i.e. Farr in Sutherlandshire.

8th November, 1825
Mr Hay and a land surveyor from Aberdeen hath been measuring and drawing a plan of the road from Daviot to the place [and] the ground that was travelled over by Allan and McKay when the former assaulted the latter, and I understand they are to take a plan of the road from here to Maclarry the morrow. It has been supposed this sometime back that Allan is wishing his trial brought on before the spring circuit and we hear he is to be taken to Edinburgh, which will give a few of us Fyvie folks a sight of that place.

30th November, 1825
Observes in the *Journal* of this day that William Allan, the person apprehended and brought here for robbery and murder last September, has received indictment to be tried at Edinburgh, 27 December. Something of this has been talked of for some time and now appears to be the case, which will let some Fyvie folks see Edinburgh.

9th December, 1825
This morning received (myself and wife) per Mr John Fyfe, messenger, summonses to appear at Edinburgh on Tuesday the 27th inst. as witnesses on the trial of William Allan. There is a good number of more folks in and about this neighbourhood that I may perhaps afterwards take a list of, this being a rather more interesting case than generally occurs at Fyvie. My wife being near the time of her confinement have caused the doctor give a certificate to that effect,

and wrote an Adam Rolland Esq., Crown Agent, Edinburgh, to have her relieved. Mr Fyfe advised this method.

23rd December, 1825
Set out from Aberdeen this morning with twelve people besides myself on a coach called the Strathmore Telegraph. Breakfasted at Stonehaven, 1/3 each; dinner at Forfar, 2/- each; and 2/- for each mutchkin toddy. Arrived in Perth about half past eight o'clock. The fare for thirteen of us from Aberdeen to Perth through Strathmore, £15.8/-, about 24/- each. Lodged at Perth in the Thane of Fife Inn, James Stewart, No. 2 Princes Street. The other seven lodge in a Mr Maxwell's, Canal Terrace.

24th December, 1825
Left Perth at nine o'clock. Went by Kinross and Queensferry. Arrived in Edinburgh about half past three afternoon. Fare from Perth to Edinburgh 9/- outside and 13/- inside. Was lodged at Edinburgh in a house near the Register Office called the Guildford Arms—J. Colson—and was very well lodged.

25th December, 1825
About eleven o'clock when we had got breakfast and in dress went out and walked in the streets—at which we was all tired out before night, every street and corner presenting something new. Went into a church at even. I think they were seceders. However, he preached well and the house was very full. It was I think in Nicolson Street.

26th December, 1825
This morning we renewed our excursions, only that we divided ourselves into two parties. That which I was in, after viewing some of the principal buildings, went to the castle, saw the Scots crown, sword and sceptre, armoury, etc. Next course was to Holyroodhouse, saw Queen Mary's apartments, pictures of all the Scottish kings, royal apartments and state rooms, where the king on his late visit held his levee and privy council. These apartments were the finest and most superb I ever saw. The pictures nearly as natural as life. In the evening went to the theatre, Rob Roy was performed and a farce called Jocco, being mostly exploits of a little man who personated a monkey. This closed our second day in Edinburgh. The reason for having two spare days in Edinburgh was in consequence of Sunday

being so near the court day and there being no stage coaches on Sunday we thought it advisable to be there on Saturday.

27th December, 1825
This day the trial of Allan came on. We were all at the courthouse by about half past ten o'clock, and perhaps about thirty of us locked up. The trial lasted from about half past ten forenoon until about eight at night. Sentenced to be executed at Aberdeen 10th February and his body given for public dissection. Our company waited the issue of the trial notwithstanding the evidences being all given in by five or six o'clock.
I went to the clerk of the coach office and engaged with him to set twelve of us down in Aberdeen for £17. The fare charged was 30/- each all outside and one pound abated on the whole. This closed our third day in Edinburgh. The weather during our stay has been favourable, being fair and frosty.

28th December, 1825
This morning after settling our bill at Edinburgh, which was £14.5/- for thirteen people three days, we set out on our journey. Nine of the party I belonged to were taken up at nine and the other three at ten. Was all in Perth (by Queensferry and Kinross) about half past three afternoon, and lodged in the same quarters as we did when going south. The weather still keeps fair and we have felt no other inconvenience but cold.

29th December, 1825
Left Perth this morning at 6 o'clock by a coach called the Cowburg (it being the Waterloo and Union that brought us from Edinburgh). Arrived at Dundee to breakfast, preferring the coast side road as we went by the Strathmore road going out. Came on by Arbroath, Montrose and Bervie, where the coach stopped to dine. Our party sought no dinner as the people on these roads make so outrageous charges. Was in Aberdeen about nine at night, all cold and wearied with the long confinement. The greater number of our party met after our arrival at the house of a James Anderson, North Street, when we gave up our partnership. The party put themselves under my charge, that is I paid all bills and also received the payment of the party who went together, consisting of thirteen up and twelve down. We was paid coach fare up and down and 7/6 a day each for

maintenance, which amounted to £8.11.10 each, and at the end of the journey at Aberdeen I gave each £2.17/- and A. Thomson who left us at Edinburgh £4.17/-, all expenses being clear.

30th December, 1825

This morning I called on some of my Aberdeen merchants and paid away the money I had left. Took a seat on the mail coach and was home here at Fyvie between two and three o'clock afternoon, and was happy when I found my family all well. Several of my neighbours came in about to welcome me home—Alex Pratt, Mill of Macterry, and Mary Duncan, one of my late servant maids, accompanied me on the coach from Old Meldrum. The names of those who were of my company are:

1	Sarah Rose, Toll Bar
2	Jane Bruce, Cowhill
3	Henrietta Gray, Barkburn
4	Jane Ironside, Muirfoundland
5	Mary Duguid, Kirkton, Daviot
6	Mary Duncan, lately at Lewes of Fyvie
7	Alex Pratt, Mill of Macterry
8	James Singer, Old Boghead
9	Adam Thomson, Mill of Burns
10	William Cran, Springleys
11	Alex Ferguson, Cairnhill of Petty
12	Alex Strachan, herd at Cowhill

and Adam Mackie, Lewes of Fyvie, brought up the rear. These all went out with one coach, and with the exception of Adam Thomson, who left us at Edinburgh, came all to Aberdeen in company. My wife was also summoned but in consequence of the doctor's certificate of being near her confinement she did not go. Some few more of the witnesses got off from indisposition. There were above forty attended, and amongst them the minister of Farr and two others from that parish in Sutherlandshire.

3rd January, 1826

Of domestic occurrences, the murder and robbery committed in this neighbourhood, with the detection and conviction of the perpetrator of that crimes, has been a case more notoriously conspicuous than was ever known by the oldest inhabitant of this place. The murder was committed 17th September on the road about two or three hundred yards beyond the nearer corner of the Wood of Rothie on the Petty side—that is to say, from the eastmost corner of the wood where Milton and Petty's land meet. The actor in this scene, William Allan, who now lies under sentence of death in Aberdeen jail, is from the parish of Monquhitter at a place called Arthur's Seat there. The family he belongs to, it appear have not been but a few years there, having come to that place from the parish of [*blank*], where it seems they had not been well liked. Neither are they in their present place, as no person laments the unfortunate young man.

10th February, 1826

William Allan from the parish of Monquhitter has this day suffered at Aberdeen for the crimes of robbery and murder. It seems he had confessed his guilt of the crimes soon after his trial but showed no feeling of regret for the commission of such an enormous crime. It is said the Reverend Mr Thom and Mr Kidd, who had joined insiduous [assiduously] to promote his eternal welfare, found their efforts fruitless beyond any former example, the wretched man seeming to give himself up to a reprobate mind. However on the more immediate prospect of death the day before his execution, he showed some symptoms of penitence and wished the clergy to continue with him more steadily, which they agreed to. His resolution at last seemed to forsake him and he fainted several times in going from his cell to the scaffold.

Chapter 10

WEATHER

23rd July, 1819
Weather very hot. Thermometer 68° in the room at four afternoon.

18th August, 1819
Salted nineteen casks butter. It is uncommonly soft, more so than I have hitherto seen, the weather is so intensely hot and dry. The crop it is feared will not be well filled in this neighbourhood, the drought has been so severe the summer throughout.

20th August, 1819
Weather exceeding hot. 72° yesterday afternoon in the house.

22nd August, 1819
The heat and drought is more extraordinary than I have ever hitherto seen. A comet is said to be in about conjunction with the sun.

30th August, 1819
The weather glass is down a fourth part since yesterday morning from thirty to twenty-nine. Bad weather anticipated. This a fine dry harvest day.

31st August, 1819
The day is dry throughout but cloudy in the afternoon with several loud claps of thunder. Lightening at night.

28th December, 1819
Storm increasing. Is very deep, I think from twelve to fifteen inches all over. My man at Littlefolla for butter, two horse in one cart, says the snow came to the bottom of the cart at even.

29th December, 1819
Storm very deep and increasing. Wind moderate from North.

30th December, 1819
A most terrible frosty day, the severest of the season. Ink frozen on desk before me.

31st December, 1819
Storm continues to increase. Frost not so intense . . . A very stormy day, am much afraid for my cart at Aberdeen . . . Storm knee deep.

1st January, 1820
This year has begun in the heart of a most terrible storm, this day and the bypast night being more severe than any of the preceding. This morning I went to James Carl and sent him away at eleven to meet my carts with two trace horses to help them home from Aberdeen. Wreaths of snow in some places shoulder high, and to speak in moderation is about two feet deep over all. Carts arrive from Aberdeen about nine at night. Men and horses much exhausted. Five double carts in town from Fyvie Castle, left three of these carts at T.B's, one mile north of Old Meldrum. Took home two carts with four horses each cart.

2nd January, 1820
A very cold day. Frost intense. No snow fallen since yesterday. I have been at church, but no great throng there. People going on the dyke tops—snow level with them. Where there was no dyke went all in a string in a narrow path like a ditch.

3rd January, 1820
Frost still severe. No alteration in the storm. Mail coach going with six horses since Saturday.

18th January, 1820
Frost terribly intense. Beer freezes on table before me at dinner this day.

19th January, 1820
This forenoon reading Journal. A few remarkable occurrences. Thermometer about a week ago stood at 7° west of Scotland. On the Clyde, horses and carts passing on the ice. Frost severe here and storm increasing.

30th January, 1821
Weather continues dry but a most terrible wind this morning and bypast night. Two of my hives have overturned, one of them much injured. A ruck set off its feet and a piece of the barn thatch blown off.

1st March, 1821
Storm continues this day with nearly the same fury as yesterday. Snow showers has been frequent with high wind from East. Nothing can be done outdoors. Weather through the winter has been most uncommonly fine, nearly like summer, and it has been generally feared that there would be some severity in spring for so mild a winter. The present confirms the supposition. The morrow is the day I should go to Auchterless but have no thought of attempting it.

4th March, 1821
A most uncommon bad day, being one continued shower of thick sleet from the east.

4th March, 1822
The present season of drought would be considered inconvenient if in the middle of summer. The sand and dust are drifting on the roads as thick as ever I saw it.

5th March, 1822
The weather is terribly boisterous, so much so that this afternoon sand and small stones are drifting about the doors like a thick shower of hail.

15th January, 1823
There has been a considerable fall of snow the bypast night and has increased this day.

16th January, 1823
The snow has increased greatly the bypast night and this day is now about nine inches deep all over.

17th January, 1823
The storm continues to increase. In some places one foot deep.

18th January, 1823
This day I have allowed to pass doing nothing. The present weather is so stormy and cold that it casts an additional damp over my native indolence so, that this day is spent doing little or nothing. The storm continues increasing and will now be about eighteen inches deep, and in some places in the country is said to be two or three feet deep. The mail coaches both from south and north are fully three hours behind their ordinary time.

23rd January, 1823
No further snow today, but at night a most terrible frost—the nails and sneck of doors are white inside.

24th January, 1823
There has been no additional snow this last two days, but the frost getting more severe. The beer and milk within doors are frozen. There has not been such a frost this three years since the end of 1819 and beginning of 1820. There was the double of the snow on the ground at that time that there is at present, but I think the frost is approaching to the same severity.

25th January, 1823
The storm continues the same with the frost intense. The sprits of wine in the thermometer of my weather glass stood at 32°, the freezing point, this morning. The frost though still strong is not so severe this night as it was yesterday night. From accounts in

the newspapers the thermometer has during the last two days stood as low as 20°. I think there has been no such frost this three years.

29th January, 1823

This is a soft day with a thick white kind of mist . . . The fog continues to even[ing], the freshness is supposed not to be permanent from the thick white mist that surrounds us with a rather unpleasant smell.

3rd February, 1823

This morning the storm is still increased and very deep now. Wreaths are from four to six feet deep and has every appearance of a growing storm. Have ranked out man with a cart and two horses to take home my wife from Old Meldrum, and from tempestuousness of the day looks to be a difficult work, the snow being deep and drifting terribly . . . Have done nothing this day but my shopkeeping and the weather has been such a continuous tempest that unless what was necessary it was improper to be out.

4th February, 1823

The storm is still increasing, although not with the same violence as yesterday . . . The storm has moderated greatly this day, but no freshness. The turnpike road it appears is nearly closed in some places. There was no south mail here yesterday, neither is there any as yet up to this time, nine o'clock pm. The road to the north is more clear. We hear the mail that went south yesterday is not further than Whiterashes.

5th February, 1823

The storm at present claims first attention. It is now more moderate but increasing. The weather has cleared up a little this day and is gone to the frost, severely more so than it has been any time this winter, if we may judge from appearances within doors. It would appear the storm to the south is still deeper than it is here. There has a mail come up from Aberdeen this day, the first since Sunday, but without the London or Edinburgh mails, three of which are due here this evening, a circumstance unprecedented in my recollection. From the settled state of the weather this day we may expect that roads will soon be cleared.

6th February, 1823

The storm continues with increased violence. A brisk wind has got up this day from the east and is driving the snow in wreaths of great deepness. I have received the *Aberdeen Journal* this day, being about twenty hours later than ordinary, from which it appears the storm is general. The frost the bypast night was the most severe during the season. We are getting no outdoor work done.

7th February, 1823

The storm which has been increasing since the evening of Saturday last has turned out a hurricane that I imagine has scarcely a parallel. The tempest is so extreme that it is with difficulty that we can go over the doors, and to go against the wind is suffocating. It is only in intervals of the gust that I can see above a hundred yards out at my shop window. I do not remember to have seen wreaths of the same height. There is one collected in my back close twelve or fifteen feet in height. It stands alone and has the appearance of a house. There is another runs along the front of the house, which may be calculated at eight or nine feet deep. At this moment, twelve noon, I can just see the top of the parapet wall of the bridge from my shop window. The wind is easterly. There may be expected great havoc among the coast shipping.

Two o'clock pm. The hurricane is getting worse rather than better. The snow appears thicker and drifting more violently. The wreath in front of the house seems changing its place. I can now see more of the bridge than I did before noon. Its greatest height now is near the garden door, perhaps eight or ten feet high, nearly parallel with dyke. The well has not been seen today. The men have taken up water at the top of the bridge from the river with a bucket and rope.

Nine o'clock at night, the tempest is without interval. I shut up my shop a little after five afternoon; need not have opened it today, have had only one customer (Johnston Skene). It is difficult getting doors shut, they are so wedged with snow about the joints. We are now cased up same as if underground. What can the situation of those people be who are now the second winter in the frozen ocean looking for a North West Passage?

I have looked out but very little today. Have sometimes been reading and at other times hearing the children a lesson. I hope the gale will be over before tomorrow.

8th February, 1823

Thank God this day the wind is calmed. We have still some showers of thick snow and wreaths [such] that I do not remember of ever seeing their equal. I thought ourselves ill but some of our neighbours are worse. The snow had been about level with the top of the smith's houses, and at my father's still higher in front of his house. It is about eighteen or twenty feet high and close on the house. We have had to dig about seven or eight feet to get at our well and a kind of passage to cut into it. There is also on the back of my shop and chamber a wreath fully four feet which [I] have raked partly off. The weather is settled as much as we have got in a ruck at which, and casting snow, have been actively employed all hands.

9th February, 1823

This is a moderate enough day with some snow showers. Have been at church, which was not very throng. The path between this and Dr Argo's house is on the top of one of my dykes, the folks all the rest of the road following one another in a string in a narrow path.

10th February, 1823

This day have got some deep snow cut and set men to work to drive some black feal. It is not good work, the snow being so very deep, but we have nothing to do and the horses are better of some exercise.

11th February, 1823

This is a terrible bad day of sleet and rain. Folks could not go out.

12th February, 1823

The weather is now settled like this day and yesterday. There have been great crowds of men cutting the snow on the turnpike road. Until this day there has not been any regular post from Aberdeen since Thursday last. I received the *Chronicle* (which is commonly here at seven o'clock on Saturday evening) this morning. They are brought by people on horseback. The road is now cleared so much that the Aberdeen coach is up this evening about her ordinary time, seven o'clock, with which we have the *Aberdeen Journal*. It is observed in that paper that there are nine London mails due at Aberdeen (a similar circumstance is not remembered), the last London mail that arrived there being on Sunday the 2nd inst. The frost on Wednesday, this day week, is remarked to be so low as 9°

on the thermometer of Fahrenheit. The present storm being greater than ever I remember seeing on the ground, it is not unworthy of notice how it was felt in other places. The *Journal* says:

> During the whole of Friday, the wind blew a hurricane without parallel in these latitudes accompanied with thick snow covering the ground generally to an immense depth, and in narrow streets and confined situations drifting to a height which completely blocked them up. We look forward with extreme apprehension to the consequence of this awful tempest. Indeed it is impossible to contemplate its effects both by sea and land without the most anxious alarm for those who may have been exposed to its tremendous fury, But the stoppage of communication may preclude us for some time from learning particulars. Two shepherds with their flocks of about two hundred sheep are said to have perished in the snow near Bridge of Dye and we dread to hear of similar casualties.

13th February, 1823
The weather since last night is settled up to frost, the snow is now so much saddened that we can walk on it without sinking.

20th February, 1823
I have been employed some time this forenoon reading the *Journal*. There are numberless accounts of losses of life and property in the late storm. It is generally admitted that there has not been anything like it since January 1799, a storm which I very well remember but thinks the present is the greatest I ever saw. This forenoon was also casting an entry through the wreath of snow into the garden, at the door of which it is still about 5 feet deep.

4th August, 1823
There has been a most terrible rain the bypast night. Ythan is above her banks this morning.

16th August, 1823
The weather continues damp. There is every appearance of the harvest being late. It was begun by this time last season, while at present there is not the most distant prospect of harvest sooner than two or three weeks. The following state of the weather is from the *Aberdeen Chronicle* of this date:

> The present season has remarkably differed from our preceding years for the greater part of the months, eight of which is nearly now

passed. February was so inclement and stormy that our excellent
roads so long obstructed by snow, that many then declared their
opinion that the summer would be cold and certainly so it has
proved, the average heat being considerably under that of any
summer heat for these 40 years past. Ripening we are sorry to
say has been at a stand for the last month, the sun rarely breaking
through the gloomy clouds and the quantity of rain that has fallen
during the months of June, July, and what has passed of August
has been great beyond any late example. A luxuriant crop is no
doubt upon the ground, but should our present moist and gloomy
weather continue, the grain must be deficient in quantity and we
fear of bad quality. Should we fortunately have dry sunny weather
for the remainder of the season, the crop may still be good but must
be late. It has been conjectured from the unnatural appearance of the
clouds during the summer that volcanic eruptions must somewhere
have taken place, and the motions of the mercury in barometers in
this part of the country have of late been unaccountably irregular.

15th January, 1826
Have been at church this [day], which was very thin. The storm is
deep and the frost the most severe that has been felt this some years,
so much so that every wet thing within doors is frozen, beer swelling
and breaking bottles and every other thing in proportion.

23rd June, 1826
The weather is intensely hot, more so than I ever remember to be
out in. Had great difficulty in getting butter weighed: the board heats
and much of the butter is very soft.

26th June, 1826
Have had John Ogilvie yesterday and this day cutting hay. It is not
above a half or a third of a crop, it is so terribly burnt with the
drought. Corn and bear crops are also suffering severely now. Corn
is shooting and not above four or five inches long; bear much the
same. On some hard high lying spots the crops are dried up with the
great heat to a cinder.

27th June, 1826
Butter is softer than I ever remember to see it. Can scarcely be
prevented running into oil. The heat continues to be strong in the

extreme. The roads are deep with dust and a cart, when there is the least wind, has always a cloud of dust about her.

28th June, 1826
Have had some terrible loud thunder this afternoon, which was followed by a heavy shower of rain, which is very agreeable after such a burning heat and drought.

29th June, 1826
From the *Journal* it appears the heat of the sun was so great in the high districts of the county as to set on fire whins in many places.

1st July, 1826
This day has been remarkable for thunder. Throughout the whole day has kept pretty distant round our horizon until towards night about 8 o'clock when it came above our heads with tremendous claps.

5th July, 1826
Read the *Journal*—accounts of great thunder storms in different parts of the country. Some buildings and beasts injured, but as yet have not heard of any loss of human life. There seems also to be great devastation by the burning of moss and muirs from the head of Don along by the source of Dee, said to be from one to two hundred square miles.

12th July, 1826
Weather continues warm and dry. Read the *Aberdeen Journal* no news of any importance other than complaints from all quarters on the dryness of the weather. The Kincardineshire agricultural report for June begins with: 'And the month has now passed by with scarcely a drop of rain, which is now the fourth in regular succession since the weather set in steadily dry'.

24th November, 1826
Went out this morning on my Auchterless journey. Had not proceeded far when a heavy rain came on which with little intermission continued throughout the day—rather the heaviest rain I ever remember being out in. I pushed on to Newton, Alex Robb's farm, where I got shelter to man, horse and cart. Stopped there rather more than

two hours when the rain faired up a little and came home . . . Came on a deep snow in the course of the evening.

25th November, 1826
If the weather was ill yesterday, it was worse this day. It has blown from north west one continued hurricane of soft sleety snow so that it has been with the greatest difficulty that people could go out.

30th November, 1826
The storm of Saturday last has blown over an extraordinary quantity of fine big trees. The sun was eclipsed visible yesterday.

2nd December, 1826
Have been back at the wood today and both my folks and horses drawing out trees. Have taken out two or three dozen . . . Reading news. This day week and preceding Friday has been terribly fatal, both on sea and shore. Great havoc all along the east coast and more especially the Moray Firth. The loss of life and property has been most severe.

23rd October, 1827
The weather was dark and wet this morning, but as I had all my goods made up ready for travel did not like to put it off. But the weather instead of fairing grew still worse and worse. I do not remember ever being out in such a bad day. The rain poured out the whole day without intermission. Man and beast was about worn out toiling from 6 morning to 10 night.

29th October, 1827
By accounts in the different newspapers Tuesday last, the day I was in Forgue, had been a storm of wind and rain all round the east coast. The Dee at Aberdeen has not been so high since 1799, and considerable damage done among shipping in the harbour. At Leith the water rose to a greater height than was ever known, the waves of the Forth dashing to the tops of the houses, and upwards of 150 sail of shipping in the Firth run up above Queensferry for shelter.

PART IV

The Wider World: A Fyvie Perspective

5.   Where Adam paid his rent. Fyvie Castle

Chapter 11

PUBLIC AFFAIRS:
POLITICS AND ECONOMICS,
ROYALTY AND CRIMINALS

3rd February, 1820
Have advice this morning that the king [George III] is dead, being about eighty-two years old and fifty-six [*recte*, sixty] a king. A few days before had advice of the death of the Duke of Kent—the king's fourth son.

20th February, 1820
At kirk as usual. A kind of funeral service for our late king, when just mentioned that he had paid the debt of nature, which we all sooner or later have to do.

1st March, 1820
Reading the *Journal* this afternoon. A great conspiracy discovered in London—intend to have assassinated all the cabinet ministers.

12th July, 1820
Employed in my shop in the morning; looking over the newspapers in the forenoon. The queen [Queen Caroline] is the present topic of public consideration—is to be put on trial of being guilty of adultery and other licentious conduct abroad in Italy.

23rd August, 1820
Reading the newspapers. The queen's trial for adultery is the present most important point. Began the 17th instant. There is much contention concerning her case. The popular party is on her side, but it is feared she will be found guilty.

3rd September, 1820

Read the *Aberdeen Chronicle* this morning on the queen's case. The trial is going on and as far as I can judge looks as if it is going against her. The witnesses' evidences are amusing. At kirk lecture . . .

6th September 1820

Read part of *Aberdeen Journal* today. Queen's trial the most important point. It would appear she has been a woman of bad morals and most irregular conduct, especially in the course of her travels abroad. Her amours with Borgami, her gallant, are of the most delicate and licentious kind.

17th September, 1820

Had a look at the *Aberdeen Chronicle* this morning. The queen's trial continues the most important point. It cannot yet be said what will be the termination. The popular clamour is on her side that she will not get justice.

21st September, 1820

By the *Journal* this week it appears the examinations of the witness against the queen are closed, when it is contended there is evidence sufficient to have proved the crime ten times in any ordinary case. Her counsel requires three weeks to bring in witness and begin her defence. He is granted this time by the Lords, when we may expect to hear little during that time.

24th September, 1820

By the papers today there is not much said about the queen as usual. The *Chronicle*, being an opposition paper, is rather on the wrong side at present, the queen's party being left with little to say if they abide by truth. In the *Chronicle* James Ferguson's death is mentioned. He was member [of parliament] for the county of Aberdeen. It was said of him that he possessed a sound judgement, which he committed to the keeping of ministers, and in return he never wanted for posts and places to the sons and nephews of his constituents.

15th October, 1820

Have been considerably engaged reading the queen's trial from the *Chronicle*. Her defence had begun in from the 3rd inst. From the examination of her witness, it would appear she would be acquitted of the charges against her. The popular clamour is still on her side.

22nd October, 1820
Read the *Aberdeen Chronicle* this day, the queen's case the most important point. Her defence are going on and there is much contradiction. It is beginning to be said that ministers will withdraw the prosecution, but of this we cannot judge aright yet. The public clamour is still on her side.

29th October, 1820
Read the Chronicle this morning. Trial of the queen occupies most attention. The examination of witness is said to be closed, and it now remains to be heard what sentence the judges will pronounce from the evidence heard from both sides.

5th November, 1820
Have read the papers this day. Full of debate on the queen's trial. It is now supposed the Bill of Pains and Penalties (as it is designated) that has been instituted against her will not pass the House of Lords, before whom the enquiry has been as yet confined. She has been guilty of some levity and improper conduct. She has been however ill used, several instances of subornation and perjury being proved in the course of the trial. There is no sentence yet.

8th November, 1820
Have read the *Journal* this day. Nearly full of pleadings on the queen's trial. There is no sentence yet. The attorney general concludes his speech with the following words (27th October—Friday):

> My Lords, The honour and dignity of the crown will be best preserved by your pronouncing a verdict according to the evidence before you. I have no doubt but that verdict will be that of guilty, which I think will be satisfactory to your consciences and sooner or later to the country at large.

There is news arrived [that] two discovery ships that have been out eighteen months in search of a north west passage to the Pacific Ocean were 115° west longitude in 70° north.

15th November, 1820
By the *Journal* this day the bill against the queen is read a second time: majority against her, twenty-eight. Also account of there being a majority of nine for it being read a third time for her degradation and divorce, but on account of the smallness of this majority, the minister proposed to give up the prosecution for six months, which was agreed to. This considered as an acquittal.

17th November, 1820
I scarcely got all my business done in Aberdeen on account of an illumination that took place in the evening on account of Her Majesty's acquittal. Cheese are unsaleable.

19th November, 1820
Have been in kirk this day . . . The most conspicuous part of this day's service was a small digression from the set form of afternoon prayer on account of the queen's acquittal. During the enquiry into the queen's conduct her name was struck out of the Church [of England's] liturgy, and from that example many of Scots ministers omitted her name also. But Mr Falconer, our minister, has always included her. His prayer for her this day was nearly to the following effect:

> We desire in a particular manner to thank Thee that Thou hast interposed to defeat the designs of the inveterate enemies of our magnanimous and benevolent queen. Be Thou ever with her and protect her, and may she live thankful unto Thee who hath delivered her from those that went about to destroy her, and may she be long preserved as an ornament and a blessing to the nation. We implore Thy blessing on that independent Church [of Scotland] whose services are not confined to forms of liturgy, who can without restraint send up their prayers unto Thee on behalf of any injured or oppressed individual. Be Thou a wall of fire about our Zion and Glory in the midst of her.

26th November, 1820
Have read the *Chronicle* this morning. Full of rejoicings in different parts of the country on account of the queen's victory, as it is called. Our minister's last week's prayer for the queen is quoted in the *Chronicle* by some person who writes it to show that the clergy are not all averse to the good cause. His sermon ran much on her

affairs this day. It was determined, says he, before she arrived in this country that she should never reign on earth, and that we were forbidden to pray for her that she might never enter into heaven. But to the upright heart and pure God will show mercy, though the hand of power, armed with the wealth of the nation and the villainy of Hell!! were lifted against her. They were all found insufficient to crush one innocent individual.

3rd December, 1820

Read the *Chronicle* this morning of queen's affairs. Still the leading point, from her being refused a palace suitable to her rank by ministers until the Commons in parliament shall make that provision for her, the Commons having just met by appointment and again [been] dismissed until the 23rd January. This raises apprehensions amongst the queen's friends that there is something now meditating against her.

25th February, 1821

Read the *Chronicle* this morning. News is of little importance. The queen business seems to be settled. She is not allowed to be prayed for by the Church of England, neither is she allowed to lodge in any of the royal palaces of England, but is allowed a salary of £50,000 a year—on which I think she may make herself comfortable, but which she seems to refuse unless her name be mentioned in the liturgy of the church.

19th July, 1821

This is the day appointed for the coronation of his present majesty, George IV. Great rejoicings at Aberdeen and other towns.

22nd July, 1821

Read the *Chronicle* this morning. The coronation rejoicing at Aberdeen and other country burghs are the principal news, with some stories about the death, burial, and character of Bonaparte, prisoner at St Helena, late Emperor of France etc.

5th August, 1821

Read *Chronicle*. Different opinions in consequence of the coronation and the rejoicings in consequence of the queen not being admitted. Her party are displeased and say the coronation is or has only been [a] useless but expensive pageant.

19th August, 1821

Read *Chronicle* this day. Are nearly full of the particulars of the queen's death, who died the 7th inst. after a few days' illness. Also of the king's visit to Ireland.

26th August, 1821

Read the *Chronicle* this morning. Nearly full about the queen's funeral procession and the obstructions it met with in consequence of taking a private route not approved of the populace. Some lives lost.

29th August, 1821

Read news today the *Journal*. The principal subject is the king's public entry into Dublin. The loyalty and splendour with which he is received there is said to baffle all description

4th November, 1821

Read the *Chronicle*. No news of importance. The king is at Hanover on a visit to his subjects there.

16th November, 1821

An execution at Aberdeen this day of a George Thom for the murder of his brother-in-law in order to get his estate.

3rd January, 1822

Myself and family has health and we enjoy peace, plenty and happiness, and all this also in a time that country people are complaining greatly . . . And although in the midst of plenty, there is room for complaint, as the produce of land will not sell at a price nearly equal to the expense of labour and rent. Hence the farmer is losing his stock. Oatmeal can be bought at present from 12/- to 12/6 the boll of 140 pounds avoirdupois. Cattle are proportionately low: two year old stots can be bought from £3 to £3.10/-, and the expense of labour and implements have suffered no deduction in proportion to produce, from all which circumstances the farming is an ill concern. It does not afford money to meet the necessary demands, much less to procure the other comforts and conveniences of life, whereby he must deny himself anything beyond the bare necessaries of life, as he must either waste his stock or run in debt. And herein the merchant suffers with the farmer in losing the profits of the retrenched articles, which was likely to be the best. But amidst all the distress that I am daily hearing I find myself comfortable, having money sufficient to meet my terms, for which I have reason to bless God above my fellows who hath made my cup to run over while others must deny themselves what they formerly indulged in. May a sense of these mercies be fixed in the mind of myself and family that we may be faithful, pious and charitable and that we may pass through this world so as to make sure of the happiness of the next.

17th April, 1822
At night read the *Journal*, from which it appears that two people had the sentence of death pronounced by the circuit court now sitting on them both for murder. The first is William Gordon, fishing tackle maker, Aberdeen, for the murder of his wife by stabbing her with a poker about the top of the thigh in January last. The other is Robert Mackintosh, farm servant, parish of Crathes, for the murder of an Elizabeth Anderson, to whom it appeared he had made some promise of marriage of which he had afterwards repented, and she was also with child by him. It appeared he had despatched her by cutting her throat dreadfully in her own bed.

31st May, 1822
This day two people have been executed at Aberdeen for the crime of murder viz. William Gordon, fishing tackle maker there, and Robert Mackintosh, farm servant from the parish of Crathes. Both admitted the justice of their sentence, and it seems were both hung up at the same time. Two executions it seems at one time is rather rare at Aberdeen, but it appears it is not the first, a William Watt and a Christian Train being executed for murder in the year 1752, that is seventy years ago.

3rd August, 1822
Read the *Aberdeen Chronicle*. The present leading article is the king's intended visit to Edinburgh and the great preparations being made there for his reception.

17th August, 1822
Read in the *Chronicle* the king's arrival at Edinburgh on the 15th inst. Also the death of the Marquis of Londonderry [Robert Stewart, Viscount Castlereagh] by his own hand.

21st August, 1822

Read the *Aberdeen Journal* at night. The leading article therein is the king's arrival at Edinburgh, the grand processions and levees with every demonstration of joy and rejoicing. The death of the Marquis of Londonderry balances the joy of the king's visit. He, Londonderry, had been seized with sudden delirium of mind, as the accounts say, and under the influence of that malady cut the great artery, left side his neck, which caused his immediate death. He filled two principal offices in the government: prime minister [*sic*] at home and Secretary of State for Foreign Affairs, and was on the eve of going out to meet the potentates of Europe in a Congress to be holden in Vienna. He is said to have been in his place in parliament on Saturday the tenth, and on Monday the twelfth committed the dreadful act. Such is the fleeting nature of human grandeur.

31st August, 1822

Read the *Chronicle* at night. The visit and departure of the king makes still the leading article, with some hints cast out respecting the magistrates of Aberdeen—that they had not met with the attention at Edinburgh they expected, but that they would bring the expense on the town's funds.

3rd January, 1823

While I am blessed with a comfortable condition, many of my fellow men are struggling as it were against the stream with the hardships of the times, which hardships are the more to be regretted as they are the effects of peace and plenty, with which the nations of Europe hath been blessed this some years. The farmer whose sole dependence is on his land at a high rent are the class of society who must soon be ruined if there is not some measures devised for their relief. The price of meal does not exceed 12/- the boll of 140 pounds avoirdupois and no ready market at that price. Cattle are proportionately low. Two year old stots from two to three pounds, three year olds from three to five pounds. These have been about the current prices during the summer markets. In the present state of things the farmer is wasting his stock or running in debt and it would appear if there is no improvement in the prices of produce that an abatement of rent can only save his ruin. My luck is that I drive a trade with some success for there is no farmer in Fyvie pays dearer for their land than I do, having twenty-five acres, some of it none the best, at

£75 sterling besides customs. Yet I find myself able to meet my terms and leave a surplus, which is to be wondered at when my principal customers, the occupiers of land, are retrenching their livings to the necessaries of life.

4th January, 1823
In the *Chronicle* at night there is a description of the two vessels, the Fury and the Hecla, that have been out since May, 1821, seeking a north west passage. They are about 380 tons each, have fifty-eight or sixty men each, and three years provisions. There are some word of the king taking another wife—a subject.

22nd May, 1823
This day there is an execution of three men at Aberdeen, a thing altogether unprecedented. Their names are Buchanan, Donaldson and McLeod, all for the crimes of housebreaking and assaulting the inhabitants.

18th October, 1823
Read the *Chronicle* at even in which there are accounts of the arrival of the Discovery ships (Fury and Hecla) at Lerwick in Shetland, where they arrived the 10th inst. after an absence of two and a half years in search of a north west passage. They had not, it appears, made great progress. The particulars are not come out.

3rd January, 1824
The farming department continues in the same languid state it has been for some years, and the farmers who during the late war with France made fortunes or had in their power to do so are now the most distressed. Grain being then on an average of 30/- the boll and cattle proportionately dear, these high prices of produce made such a run for land that rents as the farm leases wore out were doubled and in many instances trebled. When now with this heavy burden on his head and prices the half lower in these times of peace and plenty . . . the farmer is much distressed to meet his terms. And it is scarcely thought there is one who hath taken land during the last ten years and depending solely on it but what is wasting his stock or running in debt. My trade and house support me or I could not stand out. My land to speak in moderation is fully one third too dear being upwards of £3 an acre good and ill.

3rd January, 1825

Times for the farmer are rather more prosperous than they have been for some time back, the prices of produce having improved considerably the bygone year. There has been a good crop and meal at present meets a ready sell at from 15/- to 16/- the boll of 140 lbs avoirdupois. Cattle is also better by one third, in proof of which some beef I sold at this time went off as readily at 4½ pence as it did last season at 3 pence the pound. The weight of beef is the pound Dutch or 17½ ounces by avoirdupois. Butter is at present 14 pence the pound of twenty-eight ounces. Eggs have been 8 pence the dozen for some weeks, so on the whole things are much improved for the agriculturist.

3rd January, 1826

Times on the whole are improved for the generality. Cattle has been selling at high prices and grain finds a ready market . . . The interest of money hath within this few weeks taken a sudden and (to me) an unexpected rise. Only six months back some of the banks were giving only 2 per cent interest and none above 2½; and at this moment I believe 4 per cent can be readily got at any bank.

4th March, 1826

Read the *Chronicle* this afternoon. The principal news this some time has been that of great failures of banking and mercantile houses in England in the principal manufacturing towns and London especially. As a remedy for the recurrence of like evils, the legislature is proposing to suppress all banks' notes under five pounds, a measure which is likely to take place in England. The same is proposed to extend to Scotland after a lapse of three or four years, but the proposal seems to be opposed by all the county towns and corporations of Scotland.

25th March, 1826

The most important public news at present is with regard to the banking business of Scotland, there being a proposal by government of withdrawing from circulation all bank notes under £5. The proposal hath originated in consequence of great bank failures in England, thereby ruining poor people, the principal holders of small notes. The proposed measure is likely to pass into a law in England and the ministry seem resolved to extend the same law to Scotland, which the people of Scotland seem resolved against. The county gentlemen, the towns and corporations have petitioned against the measure, but as the bill is still in progress the parishes are not petitioning. Petitions to both houses of parliament have now been sent to this parish for signature. It hath been twice intimated in church that they lie with the schoolmaster. Great numbers have signed and so have I.

21st June, 1826

Read the *Journal* this afternoon. No news of any interest, but electioneering for a new parliament going on. Captain W. Gordon, brother of the Earl of Aberdeen, will be re-elected for this county without opposition. Mr Hume will also be returned for the Aberdeen district of burghs.

3rd January, 1827

Grain is at a good price now, but there are few that have any quantity to spare, the crop being so deficient. The country in general will also be pinched of fodder to bring through the livestock.

There has been much discussion about a corn bill or a corn law. The populous manufacturing towns of England and south of Scotland wish the duty taken off foreign grain, while the landed interest and others look to a free trade in grain as hurtful to the agriculture of our own country. They argue that by the foreigner glutting our market with his surplus stock, our farmer is ruined and consequently agriculture neglected, whereby we become in great measure dependent on foreign supply, while in the event of scarcity abroad or war the foreigner may require all his victual for home use, or in the latter case may not be allowed to sell us. It is likely the present session of parliament will make some alteration, but they will have ill pleasing both parties.

10th January, 1827

Read *Journal* at even. Death of the Duke of York is announced and a deal to say about him. He was heir apparent to the throne, being the king's oldest brother.

31st January, 1827

A great Hue and Cry from Aberdeen concerning the failure and forgeries of a David Milne there, an extensive ship owner and wholesale merchant deeply concerned in the home and foreign trade.

25th February, 1827
Signed a petition at the church to both houses of parliament for a continuation of the duties and restriction on the importation of foreign corn.

13th May, 1827
Catechised the children and read the newspapers this morning. The present leading news is a change of ministry in consequence of Mr Canning being appointed premier.

16th August, 1827
Have been reading the news, the most important of which is the rather unexpected death of Mr Canning, prime minister of England. He is almost universally lamented and appeared deserving the confidence reposed in him. Most of the public papers are half filled about his character and qualifications:

> High in fame, foremost in station, unrivalled in genius and eloquence, the favourite of his sovereign, the pride and darling of the British senate, the ornament of his country, the admiration of the world, delightful in private and domestic life. What wreath, what gem, what finishing could yet have added to his accumulated glory.

These six lines are from the London *Sun* Newspaper.

3rd January, 1828
The condition of the husbandman is not yet what I consider prosperous. Last summer some were nearly ruined by a bad crop. This season the crop is good, but the present Corn Laws keep the prices so low that I think the farmer's profits were hard enough earned.

Chapter 12

FOREIGN AFFAIRS

5th August, 1821
A sanguinary war is going on between the Turk and his Greek subjects [who have] revolted and are said to be encouraged and indirectly assisted by Alexander of Russia.

11th November, 1821
Read the news. There is said to be some appearance of rupture between Russia and the Turk.

12th December, 1821
Not a great deal of work or business done this day. Read [in] the *Journal* news of a Persian army of a hundred thousand men making war on Turkey in Armenia. This, as also the insurrection of the Greeks, is supposed to be the underhand work of Russia.

19th December, 1821
At even read the *Journal*. Russia appears still to be threatening the Turk.

6th January, 1822
Read the papers before kirk time. The only public news is the appearance of a war in the East. The Turkish Empire is attacked by the Persians as also by its own rebellious subjects the Greeks, and at the same time threatened by Russia. The downfall of the Porte is anticipated.

29th September, 1822
Have read the *Chronicle* this [morning]. There is no new thing. The war in the East between the Turks and the Greeks is still carried on with varied success. There is also some disturbance in Spain between what is called the Royal and the Constitutional party, the one for monarchical government, the other for legal.

11th December, 1822
Read the *Aberdeen Journal* . . . It would appear France has got permission from the Holy Alliance, as it is called—that is the sovereign princes of Europe—to make war on the Constitutional Party in Spain to compel them to restore the princes and priests of that country to the former plenitude of their power. Britain is the only power who is said to have withheld her consent to this war, and it is at present understood that she is to remain neutral. This country wants a foreign war to take off our produce.

14th December, 1822
From the news this evening there is still word of war between France and Spain but it appears declarations are not yet made. France seems to pause in a case so contrary to the inclinations of Britain. It would however appear that peace will not be long maintained.

6th April, 1823
Have read the *Chronicle* this morning. The leading point is the impending war between France and Spain. Both countries appear to be in an unsettled state in their own governments, and France looks ripe for a new revolution. The war on Spain is unpopular both in France and England.

23rd April, 1823
From the *Journal* at night, we observe the war between France and Spain is begun, the French having [attacked?] the Spaniard near St Sebastian on the seventh of the present month . . . The encounter is an open declaration of war.

2nd August, 1823
From the papers this week there is news of some fighting in Spain. The French have in the course of the summer overspread that country

with little or no opposition. The national representatives of Spain, called the Cortes, leaving Madrid retired to Seville, and, as the enemy advanced on that place, they withdrew to Cadiz carrying the king along with them, who it appears had made several attempts of escape, it being understood although not avowed [that] he—the king—favours the cause of the French, their intention being to restore him and the inquisition to the former plenitude of their power. The king and the Cortes are at present blockaded in Cadiz by the French, who it appears have a slender line of posts between that place and their own frontier. The fighting we have news of this week is by a division of the French army, who had taken a more westerly course towards Galicia and, advancing on Corunna, are opposed entering that place by the Spaniard, who was commanded by a General Quiroga assisted by an English General, Sir Robert Wilson, and a Colonel Light. The attack had been on the 15th, 16th, and 17th July. By the latest accounts the place still held out, but the Spaniards and their English general (who was wounded) had been forced to retire within the town.

18th October, 1823
Read the *Chronicle* at even . . . By the same paper is also news from Spain of the submission of Cadiz to the French, the last stronghold of the Constitutional Government, and the king was given up, who it is said will immediately repair to Madrid and be restored to all the plenitude of his power, which was an absolute despot. The Spaniards have scarcely drawn one heavy blow in the cause of independence. They are a set of treacherous cowards.

22nd October, 1823
Read the *Journal* in the evening. The leading news is from Spain, where it would appear there is great rejoicing etc. on account of the king being set at liberty by the Constitutional Government. In a proclamation the king says he disannuls [*sic*] all acts of the Constitutional Government from May, 1820 to October, 1823, declaring that during that period he had been deprived of liberty and obliged to sanction laws and authorise orders to be executed against his will, that the most criminal treason, the most disgraceful baseness, the most horrid offences had been done against his royal person. Now about to commence his return to Madrid, all members of the government called constitutional and all holding offices under

it are forbidden to come within five leagues of his route, and never to come within fifteen leagues of Madrid, and be banished the royal presence for ever. The state of the country is said to be dreadful beyond description, in anarchy, confusion and bloodshed

3rd January, 1824

Public events of the bygone year are not very important. Our own country at peace, we have only been entertained with the commotions of others. Spain has chiefly supplied the public news. Ferdinand VII of that country has been restored to absolute authority by the assistance of the French, having put down the Constitutional Government established there with the consent of prince and people since 1820 . . . The news now consists of political speculations regarding the Spanish revolted colonies of South America—whether the Holy Alliance will assist Ferdinand to restore these colonies to his allegiance. There are various opinions on the subject. England (at peace with Spain and the members of the Holy Alliance) hath sent out consuls to take care of her trade to some of the chief towns of the Spanish revolted colonies, thereby tacitly recognising the independence of the colonies. The question now is whether England will assist the colonies if old Spain and the Holy Allies shall attempt their subjugation.

While England appears to stand aloof both in words and actions, the president of the United States of America (a James Monroe) at the meeting of the States's Congress speaks out the intentions of that country, saying that the States have stood neuter during the contests of the European powers and shall still do so if they keep their own side the water, that if old Spain thinks of subjugating her revolted colonies of South America they, the United States, will permit the attempt, being convinced that the colonies are able to defend [themselves against] any attack that can be made on them by old Spain in her present enfeebled state: but that if any other European power shall interfere to give Spain assistance in that subjugation they, the United States, will consider such interference unfriendly to them and will not remain spectators to the Holy Alliance of Europe planting despotic governments on the American hemisphere, which might spread to themselves, whose government they know is not very amicable to these allies. Thus the United States speak out what the English dissemble. The thing is manly and sets the New World in the place of dictator to the old.

18th September, 1824
In the *Chronicle* at night is mentioned the death of Louis XVIII, King of France. He was an old infirm man.

3rd January, 1826
The close of the year has also closed the life of Alexander, Emperor of Russia, the greatest prince in Europe, if not the greatest on earth since the fall of Bonaparte. Some political changes are expected in consequence of the change of one of the greatest princes of Europe. Constantine, brother of Alexander, it seems is the person now appointed.

4th March, 1826
There is a report in this day's paper that Nicholas, the new Emperor of Russia, is assassinated, and ninety of the chief nobility.

20th December, 1826
During the evening reading the *Journal*. Our Government is sending out some troops to Portugal to assist the Portuguese in defending some encroachment made by Spain and some Portuguese insurgents.

3rd January, 1827
From the corn laws the public attention has been drawn these some weeks to the affairs of Portugal, by our government sending out troops—about twelve or sixteen regiments—to assist the government of that country in putting down some fugitive rebels, who it would appear had taken shelter within the Spanish frontier and had been allowed and assisted by Spain to organise themselves and make war on their own country (Portugal), with a view of overturning the newly adopted Constitutional Government.

3rd January, 1828
The Turk and Greek are the only powers at war in Europe and all eyes are of late turned to that quarter in consequence of the governments of Russia, France and Britain having entered into an alliance in order to give freedom to the Greeks by using their influence with the Turk: and failing of negotiation to have recourse to arms. And to give weight to the arguments of the ambassadors each of the three Powers have sent a fleet into the Mediterranean,

the which fleets received some insult from the Turks in those seas by their firing on a boat carrying some dispatches for the commander of the Turks stationed at Navarino in the Morea, whereby it was said the commander and most of the boat's crew were killed. The consequence was that the allied fleet immediately engaged the Turks and completely destroyed their fleet consisting of seventy sail of different denominations. This took place 20th October last in the Bay of Navarino.

The negotiations with the Porte continued up to the first week of December, at which time we are told the ambassadors left Constantinople as the Grand Signior could not be prevailed on to make any concessions in favour of the Greeks. What the allies are to do next remains to be seen.

GLOSSARY

The following definitions are not comprehensive: they only define words in the senses in which they are used in Adam Mackie's diary.

anent: *concerning*
bear: *a coarse but hardy kind of barley*
ben: *in or towards.* '*Come ben*' = *come in*
bondage: *services due by a tenant to a landlord*

cags: *kegs*
chincough: *whooping cough*
claick, cliak, clyak: *the last sheaf of corn to be harvested, sometimes decorated with ribbons*

damp: *depression*
drive: *to pile or heap up*
dub, dubs: *mud*
dubbied: *muddied*

eek: *a ring of straw or wood used to enlarge a beehive*

feal: *turf*

haugh: *low lying ground or meadow*
howe: *hollow or valley*

lateron: *the precentor's desk in a church*

lose, louse: *to unharness an animal, or unpack goods*

lum: *chimney*

mart: *a cow killed and its flesh salted to provide meat during the winter*

osnaburgh: *a type of coarse linen cloth*
outcast: *quarrel*

piggery: *earthenware vessels*
posting: *writing up accounts or other records*

quey: *a heifer*

raiding, redding: *cleaning or clearing out*
raised: *excited, infuriated*
reaching: *retching*
riped: *ripened*
rose: *inflammation of the skin caused by erysipelas (a streptcoccal skin
       infection accompanied by high fever and often leading to fatal
       complications)*
roup: *auction*
ruck: *rick*

saddened: *compacted or consolidated*
shade: *shed*
shalt: *shelt or pony*
skep: *beehive*
sneck: *latch*
stitches: *sharp pains*
stot: *bullock*

tardings: *marks left on the skin after being beaten with a 'tards' or tawse
          (a leather strap)*
thacking: *thatching*
throng: *busy, crowded*
tumble: *to toss about or wander about*

walking: *watching over a corpse*
whiteiron: *iron plated with tin*
winter: *feast marking the end of the harvest*

Appendix I

INDENTURE OF APPRENTICESHIP

Indenture betwixt William Mackie and Adam Mackie, 5 years from 15ᵗʰ February, 1800

It is contracted and agreed upon between William Mackie, shoe-maker in Aberdeen, on the one part and Adam Mackie, lawful son of Adam Mackie, shoemaker in Fyvie, with consent of the said Adam Mackie, his father, on the other part in manner following:

That is to say the said Adam Mackie junior hereby binds and engages himself as an apprentice and servant to the said William Mackie in his business as aforesaid for the space of five full and complete years, from and after the fifteenth day of February last, which is hereby declared to have been the commencement of his apprenticeship, notwithstanding the date hereof. During which space the said Adam Mackie junior obliges himself to serve his said master diligently, honestly and obediently, to conceal his master's lawful secrets, to prevent his loss and damage to the utmost of his power, not to absent himself from his master's service without leave asked and obtained under the penalty of paying one shilling and sixpence sterling to his said master or serving him two days at the expiration of the present indenture, in his master's option, for each day's absence; to abstain from gaming, drinking, night walking and all idle and debauched company, and from every other immorality, and in general to behave himself in every respect as a faithful, honest and diligent servant and apprentice. For whose honesty, diligence, sure remaining at his apprenticeship and faithfully and punctually performing the premises the said Adam Mackie senior binds and obliges himself, his heir's, executors and successors, as cautioner, surety, and full debtor for and with the said Adam Mackie junior. For which causes, and on the other part, the said William Mackie obliges himself to teach and instruct the said Adam Mackie junior his apprentice in his business aforesaid as a shoemaker, and in all the branches thereof, and to conceal no part thereof from his said apprentice insofar as he himself knows or his said apprentice is capable to conceive, and he further obliges himself to maintain his said apprentice in bed and board during his apprenticeship, either in his own house or elsewhere in the master's option, and to maintain him in shoes during the whole of his apprenticeship.

Lastly both parties bind and oblige themselves mutually to perform the premises to each other under the penalty of ten pounds sterling to be paid by the party failing to the party performing or willing to perform over and above performance. And for the more security they consent to the registration hereof in the Books of Council and Session or any other competent register, that letters of horning on six days charge and all other execution necessary may pass thereupon in common form. For which purpose they constitute their procurators. In witness whereof they have subscribed these presents (written by George Yeats, writer in Aberdeen, on this sheet of stamped paper) at Aberdeen, the nineteenth day of September eighteen hundred years before witnesses John Wallace shoemaker in Aberdeen, and the said George Yeats.

John Wallace	Witness	*William Mackie*
Geo. Yeats	Witness	*Adam Mackie* senior
		Adam Mackie junior

Aberdeen 15 February 1805. This is to certify that the within mentioned Adam Mackie junior has served me the within mentioned five years honestly and faithfully as an apprentice, of which he is hereby discharged by

William Mackie

Appendix II

THE TRIAL OF WILLIAM ALLAN
FOR MURDER

Trial of William Allan before the High Court of Justiciary, Edinburgh
1825

Medical Evidence
There was a depressed fracture of the right parietal bone above and
behind the right ear, in the form of a letter T, 2" long from back to
front and 3" broad from above down. The brain was seen pulsating
and parts of it were lying on his hair and on the shoulder of his coat.
The dura mater was lacerated. Blood was oozing from the wound
and right ear and mouth. By enlarging the wound I succeeded in
extracting four pieces of bone and several small spiculae. There was
a small wound behind the lower part of the right ear ½" long and one
in front of the right ear on the cheek about 1" in length. There was
another wound at the external angle of the right eye and another on
the left cheek. The middle of the nose was slightly injured and skin
on other parts of the face abraded. The 4th rib on the right side
was fractured and there were several livid spots over the same side.
Breathing was difficult. These injuries could not have been caused
by a fall. He answers questions rationally. He feels sick and says
his head is dizzy. His face and lips are pale. He is shivering, the
pulse is slower than normal and very weak. From this examination,
I consider the man's life in imminent danger. J. Chalmers, surgeon.
(Report confirmed by Dr Thomas Pirie, surgeon).
 The post mortem report confirmed the earlier report.

 Dr Blaikie, MD., examined Allan as to his mental condition. He
considered him to be of sound mind. Allan was at first advised to
feign madness, but later said he had been ill-advised.

Sentence

The Lord Justice Clerk and the Lords Commissioners of Justiciary, in respect of the verdict [of guilty], discern and adjudge the said William Allan, panel, to be carried from the bar to the jail of Edinburgh, therein to be detained until delivered over by the magistrates of Edinburgh to John Fife, messenger at arms in Aberdeen, to be by him to be transmitted under a sure guard till he is brought to and incarcerated in the tolbooth of Aberdeen, therein to be detained and fed on bread and water only in terms of the act of Parliament passed in the 25th year in the reign of His Majesty King George the Second instituted as 'an act for preventing the horrid crime of murder', until Friday the tenth day of February next to come, and upon that day between the hours of two and four o'clock to be taken furth of the said tolbooth to the common place of execution within the burgh of Aberdeen, and there to be hanged by the neck on a gibbet by the hands of the common executioner until he be dead, and his body thereafter to be delivered to the Professor of Anatomy in the University of Aberdeen, to be by him publicly dissected and anatomized in terms of the said act; and ordain his whole moveable goods and gear to be escheat and inbrought to His Majesty's use, which is pronounced for doom.